Praise for
A CONVERT.

M000028071

"*A Converted Woman's Voice* includes so many gems of truth that resonate with me personally—as a woman and as a member of the Church of Jesus Christ of Latter-day Saints. Maria's book is filled with valuable insights and inspired ways to share our voices and hearts!"

— Si Foster, creator of the food blog, *A Bountiful Kitchen*

"The voice of a converted woman is needed now more than ever."

— Brad Wilcox, author of *The Continuous Atonement*

"Every Latter-day Saint woman seeks purpose and mission. Maria's brilliant book enables us to filter out 'thin things' as converted women in order to concentrate on what the world needs, while encouraging us to elevate our thinking and magnify our voices as we clarify our plans. You will feel enlightened while reading this book!"

— Nikki Eberhardt, Assistant Professor
at Minerva Business College

"I must say, this book is extraordinary! It is truly exceptional. So profoundly insightful. I could not put it down. It is filled with great wisdom, insight, examples, and stories."

— Stephen M.R. Covey, author of the *New York Times* bestselling, *The Speed of Trust*, and *Smart Trust*

"The Spirit-changing process of reading *A Converted Woman's Voice* has blessed my life. Maria's book is filled with the Spirit, evidence of Heavenly Father and the Savior's great love for us, and motivation to align to a greater degree with our Heavenly Father's plan. It is personal, brave, easily understood, well-organized, flowing, poetic, true."

— Wendy Moosman, ward Relief Society president

"I appreciate Maria's thoughtful insights regarding the gospel and life. She shares powerful stories and real-life examples of principles that are sorely needed. I believe this book can be a great benefit to Latter-day Saints, especially Latter-day Saint women."

— Scott Esplin, BYU Religious Studies Center

Keep sharing your converted voice!
♡ *Maria*

A Converted Woman's Voice

Being Valiant in the Testimony of Jesus
and in His Restored Gospel

Maria Covey Cole

atmosphere press

For my magnificent husband, Dave,
"a man after mine own heart"—
with love

No one can defend our Savior with any more persuasion or power than you—the daughters of God. You have such inner strength and conviction. The power of a converted woman's voice is immeasurable, and the Church needs your voices now more than ever.

—M. Russell Ballard, "Let Us Think Straight,"
BYU Speeches, Aug. 20, 2013

Contents

Introduction

When thou art converted, strengthen thy brethren [and sisters].

— Luke 22:32

I keep two postcard-sized prints in my desk drawer which I try to look at every day. One is a depiction of the Savior, the Good Shepherd, who watches attentively over his beloved sheep herd. Another is a portrayal of the boy Joseph Smith as he kneels in the Sacred Grove—a pillar of light illuminating his face. To me, these images represent the essence of my testimony of Jesus Christ and His restored gospel.

I came to this testimony as a young girl—*I have always believed*—but it was greatly fortified as an adult one afternoon while watching "The Testaments," in the Legacy Theatre of the Joseph Smith Memorial Building. As clear as day, the Spirit bore witness to my soul, and my personal mission was revealed to me: "To be valiant in the testimony of Jesus and in His restored gospel."

Several years ago, I attended Education Week at Brigham Young University (BYU) for the express purpose of finding out how God wanted me to use my time and talents. I was at a crossroads . . . my five children, who had needed me so desperately when they were younger, were now becoming more independent—a few had even left the home—and I desired to receive direction as to how to spend my time at this stage of my life. In addition to being a homemaker, I was teaching a writing class at a private college and doing some freelance editing, but I felt deeply that I was supposed to be doing something more.

Elder M. Russell Ballard gave the keynote speech at the opening session, and he told about his recent visit to the British Isles, where he toured some of the missions, met the members there, and visited Church history sights. He had been profoundly affected by this trip, and especially by the legacy of faith demonstrated by the British Saints.

In remembering the early Saints who joined the Church in Great Britain, Elder Ballard was particularly impressed with the sisters who acted so valiantly in embracing the gospel and facilitating their family's immigration to America. History has shown that the power and influence of these faithful women strengthened the Saints and literally saved the Church in its infancy.

When these immigrant families made their way to Nauvoo, Illinois, their grit and determination was a boon to the body of the Saints who had been worn down by persecution, poverty, and hardship. These British immigrants further served to bolster the handcart companies on their pioneer trek to Salt Lake City.

Elder Ballard then applied these lessons to the Latter-day Saint sisters sitting in that Education Week audience. He stated: "The same is true now. In so many ways, women are the heart of the Church." He went on to pay tribute to the influence of strong Latter-day Saint women and the impact for good we may have upon others.

To me, the most impactful statement Elder Ballard made in his speech that day was when he affirmed the sisters of the Church in the following way:

"No one can defend our Savior with any more persuasion or power than you—the daughters of God. You have such inner strength and conviction. The power of a converted woman's voice is immeasurable, and the Church needs your voices now more than ever."[1]

When I left that opening session with Elder Ballard's charge penetrating my heart, I immediately began thinking of ways I could use my voice for good. I was a converted Latter-day Saint woman. What was the best vehicle for me to share my conversion with others? How could God use me as an instrument in His hands to bear testimony to all the world of the things I knew to be true?

Sometime later, I was studying my father's writings and I received my answer. I read: "To become an [effective] leader who makes a contribution in life, answer the following questions: *What does the world need from you? What are you good at?* And finally, *How can you best do what you like to do and meet real needs in the world or in the Church?*"[2]

When I contemplated the answers to these questions, it made me realize that what God wanted me to do was write—to use my voice for good—to share my faith and testimony, with the hope of converting and strengthening other Latter-day Saint women.

Since that time, I have felt a great responsibility to minister to the individual, to take personally the latter-day instruction: "[B]e faithful, stand in the office which I have appointed unto you; succor the weak, lift up the hands which hang down, and strengthen the feeble knees" (D&C 81:5).

Scores of spiritual impressions have flooded into my mind and heart. I cannot deny the inspiration that has been so abundantly poured out upon me. I know that Heavenly Father wants me to be valiant in my testimony of Jesus and in His restored Church by being a worthy witness of the truthfulness of the gospel, and in standing strong for motherhood, the family, and the home. This book is the result of these impressions.

Each chapter addresses a theme that is meaningful to me as a converted woman. The sequence of the topics is important in that knowledge is foundational, and we must build upon a base layer of truths before we can recognize the value of others. At the conclusion of each chapter, there are some questions to review and initiatives to consider. An *initiative* is an introductory step or a plan, which implies the ability to act on one's own. After all, faith is a principle of action and power, and it requires faith to act upon what one knows and believes.

We must never lose sight of the greater picture and the divine destiny of this work and the part each of us has to play in the grand scheme of things. Much of what we can do is to become a leader and a model of what a converted woman looks like—but first we need to become converted women ourselves.

My daughter-in-law, Kelsey, is a converted woman who is concerned that too many of us are getting caught up in the "thick of thin things." While she recognizes that many causes are worthy and important, she worries that we may become distracted and lose perspective of our true purpose, which is to champion Christ, His gospel, and our

Father's Plan of Happiness. The longer our focus is directed towards the distraction, she reasons, the easier it is for Satan to poke holes in the "stronghold" of our testimonies.

"Can you imagine the good we could do and the impact we could have if all Latter-day Saint women were motivated by the cause of Christ first and foremost, and felt equally passionate about guarding the integrity of the family and the doctrines of the Church?" Kelsey reasons.

Quoting an anonymous writer, President Harold B. Lee once said: "Survey large fields and cultivate small ones." In other words, recognize the vast scope and eternal significance of God's plan for His children, and then, as converted women of God, diligently seek to fulfill our part in that divine plan, however inconsequential our role may seem to be.

The following insight by former Young Women General President, Margaret Nadauld, gives context and meaning to our charge to become women of God:

"Women of God can never be like the women of the world. The world has enough women who are tough; we need women who are tender. There are enough women who are coarse; we need women who are kind. There are enough women who are rude; we need women who are refined. We have enough women of fame and fortune; we need more women of faith. We have enough greed; we need more goodness. We have enough vanity; we need more virtue. We have enough popularity; we need more purity."[3]

May God continue to bless us in our efforts to become converted "women of God," and then give us the resolve to reach out, open our mouths, and strengthen our fellow sisters in the gospel.

[1] M. Russell Ballard, "Let Us Think Straight," *BYU Speeches*, Aug. 20, 2013.

[2] Stephen R. Covey, *Primary Greatness*, 2015, 72.

[3] Margaret D. Nadauld, "The Joy of Womanhood," *Ensign*, Nov. 2000.

Chapter 1
Identity

What lies behind us and what lies before us are tiny matters compared to what lies within us.

— *Ralph Waldo Emerson*

A few months after returning from her mission to Preston, England, my sister, Jenny, married her college sweetheart, Jason, who had waited for her. Jason had been admitted to dental school at Marquette—a Catholic, Jesuit University, located in Milwaukee, Wisconsin. Soon after their wedding, they made the move.

Finding herself a few semesters shy of graduation, Jenny transferred her academic credits from BYU to Marquette in order to complete her English major. During her first semester at Marquette, Jenny enrolled in a philosophy class, and anticipated having religious discussions similar to the ones she'd experienced at BYU.

On the first day of class, the philosophy teacher gave a lecture introducing the subject matter the class would be studying that semester. Following a captivating prologue, he opened discussion with the following invitation:

"Have you ever asked yourselves these questions: Where did I come from? Why am I here? What will happen after I die?"

"Are you kidding me?" Jenny thought to herself. "This man is golden. He's asking all of the questions central to the purpose of life. Here is my opportunity to share the Plan of Salvation with my entire class!"

Possessed with the zeal and excitement of a recently returned missionary, Jenny looked around, and then confidently raised her hand high. Somewhat perturbed that someone would interrupt his philosophical discourse, the professor grudgingly called on her to speak.

Jenny began: "I can share the answer to those questions . . ."

She paused, and then testified: "God is our loving Heavenly Father. We are His spirit children. We lived with Him before we came to earth. We have come to earth to gain a body and to be tested to see if we are willing to walk by faith. God has a plan for our lives, and we will live with Him again after we die."

The professor coldly stared her down. Finally, he responded, "Religion . . . That's one answer . . . Anyone else?"

Jenny was flabbergasted! Was this not a religious institution? Was the teacher not sincere in his desire to learn the answer to these questions or was this just a theoretical exercise? Jenny spent the rest of the semester being contained by the professor. He rarely allowed her to speak, and when he did, he treated everything she expressed with suspicion.

Every human being carries in his or her heart questions essential to the purpose of life. *Who am I? Why am I here? Where will I go after I die?* Since the beginning of time, philosophers, scholars, and experts have spent their entire lives seeking answers to these fundamental questions.

As members of the restored Church, we are not left to wonder about these uncertainties. Rather, through latter-day revelation, we know who we are, why we are here, and what the purpose of our lives is.

Hold fast to foundational truths

In a general conference address, President Dieter F. Uchtdorf expressed appreciation for the knowledge we have been given of God's Plan of Life and Salvation:

"I am grateful that the restored gospel of Jesus Christ has answers to the most complex questions in life. These answers are taught in The Church of Jesus Christ of Latter-day Saints. They are true, plain, straightforward, and easy to understand. They are inspired, and we teach them to our three-year-old's in the Sunbeam class.

"Brothers and sisters, we are eternal beings, without beginning and without end. We have always existed. We are the literal spirit children of divine, immortal, and omnipotent Heavenly Parents!

"We come from the heavenly courts of the Lord our God. We are of the royal house of Elohim, the Most High God. We walked with Him in our premortal life. We heard Him speak, witnessed His majesty, and learned His ways."[1]

In September of 1995, President Gordon B. Hinckley first introduced the Family Proclamation during the General Relief Society meeting. In the opening paragraphs, fifteen living Apostles and prophets unanimously affirmed: "All human beings . . . are created in the image of God. Each is a beloved spirit son or daughter of heavenly parents."[2]

This document, along with the Holy Scriptures and the words of the prophets, testifies that we are the children—the literal offspring—of God, and that we have a divine nature and destiny.

"Our most fundamental doctrine includes the knowledge that we are children of a living God," states Elder Donald Hallstrom in a general conference address.[3] "This doctrine is so basic, so oft stated, and so instinctively simple that it can seem to be ordinary, when in reality it is among the most extraordinary knowledge we can obtain. A correct understanding of our heavenly heritage is essential to exaltation. It is foundational to comprehending the glorious plan of salvation and to nurturing faith in the Firstborn of the Father, Jesus the Christ, and in His merciful Atonement (see Colossians 1:13–15). Further, it provides continual motivation for us to make and keep our indispensable eternal covenants."[4]

If it is true that a correct understanding of our divine heritage is "essential," "foundational," "motivation [al]," and "indispensable" to us keeping our eternal covenants, how can we cause this most central doctrine to sink more deeply into our minds and hearts? How can we allow these truths to fundamentally change our very beings?

Adopt a gospel perspective

One answer is to look to those who have allowed these truths to change their very nature. Joseph F. Smith is an example of a person—a latter-day prophet—who had a life-changing experience around these very truths.

I have always had a special place in my heart for Joseph F. He was Hyrum and Mary Fielding Smith's son. He was born in dire circumstances in Far West, at the time the Saints were forced out of Missouri and his father and others were betrayed, arrested, and thrown in Richmond Jail.

As a six-year-old boy in Nauvoo, Joseph F. never forgot seeing his father for the last time when, on his way to Carthage on horseback, he picked up his son, kissed him, and set him down. Neither could he forget the terror of hearing a neighbor rap on the window at night to tell his mother that Hyrum and his Uncle Joseph had been killed, nor of her subsequent anguish and grief.

At nine years old, he accompanied his widowed mother, Mary Fielding, across the plains to Utah. Four years after arriving in the Salt Lake Valley, she too passed away, leaving Joseph F. an orphan at the age of 13. When he was 15, he was ordained an Elder and sent to Hawaii as a missionary. Much of the time he labored alone. He had no money. It was in these discouraging circumstances that Joseph F. received the following vision:

I was almost naked and entirely friendless, except [for] the friendship of a poor, benighted, degraded people. I felt as if I was so debased in my condition of poverty, lack of intelligence and knowledge, just a boy, that I hardly dared look. . . man in the face.

While in that condition I dreamed [one night] that I was on a journey, and I was impressed that I ought to hurry—hurry with all my might, for fear I might be too late. I rushed on my way as fast as I possibly could, and I was only conscious of having just a little bundle, a handkerchief with a small bundle wrapped in it. . . I came to a wonderful mansion. . . It seemed too large, too great, to have been made by hand, but I thought I knew that was my destination.

As I passed towards it, as fast as I could, I saw a notice [that read], "Bath." I turned aside quickly and went into the bath and washed myself clean. I opened up this little bundle that I had, and there was a pair of white, clean garments. . . and I put them on. Then I rushed to what appeared to be a great opening, or door. I knocked and the door opened, and the man who stood there was the Prophet Joseph Smith. He looked at me a little reprovingly, and the first words he said [were]: "Joseph, you are late . . ."

[I replied,] "Yes, but I am clean—I am clean!"

He clasped my hand and drew me in, then closed the great door. I felt his hand just as tangible as I ever felt the hand of man. I knew him, and when I entered I saw my father, and Brigham and Heber, and Willard, and other good men that I had known, standing in a row. . . My mother was there. . .

When I awoke that morning [alone, away up in the mountains of Hawaii] I was a man, although only a boy. There was not anything in the world that I feared. I could meet any man or woman or child and look them in the face, feeling in my soul that I was a man every whit. That vision, that manifestation and witness that I enjoyed at that time has made me what I am, if I am anything that is good, or clean, or upright before the Lord, if there is anything good in me. That has helped me out in every trial and through every difficulty. . .

. . . I felt as if I had been lifted out of a slum, out of a *despair, out of the wretched condition that I was in; and naked as I was, or as nearly as I was, I was not afraid of any . . . man . . . and I have not been very much afraid of anybody else since that time. I know that that was a reality, to show me my duty, to teach me something, and to impress upon me something that I cannot forget. I hope it never can be banished from my mind [GD, 542–43].*[5]

Joseph F. was given an understanding of who he truly was, apart from his temporal circumstances. He was a child of God, a son of noble parents, and he had a divine birthright and destiny. When he truly comprehended that he was known and loved by God and by an army of valiant spirits on the other side of the veil, it gave him the courage and strength he needed to fulfill his mission, and to go on to consecrate his life to building the Kingdom of God on the earth.

President Ezra Taft Benson explains this "inside out" phenomenon:

"The Lord works from the inside out. The world works from the outside in. The world would take people out of the slums. Christ takes the slums out of people, and then they take themselves out of the slums. The world would mold men by changing their environment. Christ changes men, who then change their environment. The world would shape human behavior, but Christ can change human nature . . .

"Yes, Christ changes men, and changed men can change the world."[6]

We found this principle to be true as we visited our daughter Hannah's mission in Dallas, Texas, where we went for a visit nine months after she had returned home.

When we tried to track down her new converts, we

could only find them with difficulty. They no longer lived in the places they had lived when Hannah found and taught them the gospel of Jesus Christ.

Those who were living in underprivileged parts of town had moved to more respectable areas; those who had been living in apartments had purchased homes. In almost every situation, each of these individuals had bettered their circumstances. Christ had taken the slums out of the people, so to speak, and then they had taken themselves out of the slums.

Comprehend your true identity and divine nature

On one occasion, my father had the opportunity to speak to the missionaries at the Missionary Training Center (MTC). As he came to the conclusion of his speech, he felt impressed to testify of the worth of each soul in attendance.

He closed by saying: "You are God's own son or daughter. He knows and loves you perfectly and personally. You are precious. You matter. You have intrinsic worth—not to be compared with any other."

Following his remarks, a line formed of missionaries who wanted to speak to him. One Elder approached and pleaded: "Would you please tell me that again—that part about me being God's own son?"

My father looked him directly in the eye and, with all the tenderness of a loving parent, testified: "You are God's own son. He loves you. You are precious in His sight—not to be compared with any other."

With tears streaming down his face, the Elder repeated his request: "Would you please tell me that again?"

Our son, Colin, had an experience analogous to my father's when he was serving his mission in Taiwan. His investigator, George, had severe depression—the worst Colin had ever seen—and he told the Elders that the only thing that would give him any relief was to smoke. George had developed a two-pack-a-day cigarette habit that he could not imagine discontinuing. He didn't understand why God would ask him to give up the one substance that helped alleviate his pain and anxiety.

Colin and his companion were very prayerful about George and his difficulty with the Word of Wisdom. They sincerely desired to know how they could help him overcome this obstacle to baptism. As they pondered upon his situation, Colin felt impressed that he should testify to George of his identity as a noble son of a loving Heavenly Father.

The next time they were together, he did so. Colin (Elder Cole) looked him directly in the face and lovingly testified: "George, you are God's own son. You are of infinite worth. He knows and loves you. You are precious in His sight. God has a plan for your life."

George was moved to tears and completely overcome by the Spirit. After their discussion, he went home, and out of habit, lit up a cigarette. As he began smoking, however, the fumes suddenly made him feel sick, and he was not even able to finish. From that day on, George completely lost his desire to smoke and hasn't touched tobacco since. He was baptized, ordained an Elder, and is currently preparing to serve a mission. Comprehending who he truly was literally gave George the spiritual strength needed to quit smoking.

We all long to know who we are and that we matter. It

is essential to our well-being and personal security to understand our true identity and heritage. We must never forget that we are in-very-deed daughters of God. He is our loving Heavenly Father who desires for us to be happy. Lasting happiness is found only in the Plan of our God and through obedience to the commandments of His Son—our Savior Jesus Christ.

God knows your name

Many years ago, my niece Victoria saw a movie entitled *Legally Blonde*, and she identified so deeply with the main character, Elle Woods, whom she considered to be spunky and cute, that she asked everyone to call her Elle, and not Victoria, from then on.

Her parents were shocked, to say the least, and a little hurt, but they decided it wasn't worth the battle and complied with her wishes. Victoria, or Elle, I should say, even legally changed her name. Every one of her family and friends began calling her Elle.

Several years went by and she decided to serve a mission. She was called to serve in the West Indies as an English-speaking missionary. Not long after she arrived in the mission field, she felt strongly that she should be speaking French, and she shared this prompting with her Mission President. At the time, he couldn't foresee the need for an additional French-speaking sister, but within a month the demand arose, and Elle was switched to the French side.

Since Elle had not learned French in the MTC, she was left on her own to figure it out. She writes of a particularly challenging time when learning the language, and how she poured out her heart to God in prayer.

She said: *"I don't know if you're hearing my prayers. I don't even know if you know who I am."*

Immediately, she heard a voice in her mind say: *"I know who you are . . . Victoria."*

This experience deeply affected and changed her, as she knew that the Lord was aware of her struggles and had reached out to her in a very personal way, calling her by her given name—a name she hadn't gone by in years. On her next preparation day, she wrote to her family, expressing gratitude that God knew who she was, had answered her prayer, and manifested His love.

She asked that everyone please start calling her Victoria again. "If God knows me by that name, then that is the name I want to go by," she explained.

Awaken the memories of the Spirit

Not long ago, I read the excellent biography of the late Truman G. Madsen, written by his son, Barney. Truman was a dear friend of our family, a BYU philosophy professor, a prolific author, a noted scholar, and a defender of the faith.

When Truman Madsen was sixteen years old, the movie *Random Harvest,* with Ronald Colman and Greer Garson, came to Salt Lake City. In those days (back in 1942), admission to the theatre cost just 15 cents, so Truman returned to see this movie five times. Although just a youth, Truman was a philosopher at heart, and he became haunted and enveloped by the themes of this film. He later explained: "[I]t is for me the allegory of our life and our dilemma."[7]

Truman goes on to recount the plot of *Random Harvest,* which is about a man who forgets who he is. First, it's the shell shock of war that destroys his identity; next, it's slipping and falling on his head and being hit by a taxi that makes him forget who he really is. Yet, in the end, he finds himself in a similar setting to where he started, and memories begin to come together as he regains his true identity.

"Well, that's exactly our dilemma. We are here not fully knowing name, rank, and serial number," Truman explains. "We are here trying to find a niche, or a mission. We have these feelings occasionally that we have known somebody, known them in other circumstances . . .

"Whatever else you make of it, we have this unusual notion that there will come a time, and I can't tell you where it will be and how, we will get our memory back, and so much will then make sense. That here has only been oblique and full of wonder. And we may even have for the first time completely a sense of our own identity: 'Yes, that's who I am.'"[8]

As Joseph F. Smith taught: "Every salient truth that comes so forcibly to the heart and mind of man is but an awakening of the memories of the Spirit."[9] We do know, but we don't know how.

The truths of the restored gospel are simple, yet profound. As we seek to study these truths, "the solemnities of eternity [will] rest upon [our] minds" (D&C 43:34) and bring us great joy. Let us draw upon the revealed knowledge that we have been blessed with as Latter-day Saint sisters and allow this revelation to lift and inspire us.

Initiatives to consider

1. You are a daughter of God. Reflect on the wondrous meaning of that one paramount fact.
2. How does knowing your true identity inspire you to become the person whom God intended you to be?
3. You are an essential part of our Heavenly Father's plan. How can you fulfill your role in His plan and tap the marvelous potential that lies within you?

---

[1] Dieter F. Uchtdorf, "O How Great the Plan of our God," *Ensign*, Nov. 2016.

[2] "The Family: A Proclamation to the World," *Ensign*, Nov. 2010.

[3] Donald L. Hallstrom, "I Am a Child of God," *Ensign*, May 2016.

[4] *Ibid.*

[5] Joseph F. Smith, *Gospel Doctrine* (Deseret Book, 1939), 542–43.

[6] Ezra T. Benson, "Born of God," *Ensign*, July 1989.

[7] Barnard Madsen, *The Truman G. Madsen Story: A Life of Study and Faith* (Deseret Book, 2016), 306

[8] *Ibid.* 306-308.

[9] Joseph F. Smith, qtd. in Stephen R. Covey, "How to Testify," *Liahona*, Nov. 1977

Chapter 2
Conversion

Knowing that the gospel is true is the essence of a testimony. Consistently being true to the gospel is the essence of conversion.

— Elder David A. Bednar

Recently, I ran into a family friend at the doctor's office. I asked about the welfare of his oldest daughter whom I had gotten to know while serving in our stake Young Women. This lovely young woman had a testimony—there was no doubt about it—but she struggled to live the commandments. The last time we'd talked, her family was extremely worried about the choices she was making.

Her father's reply was very telling. He responded: "She is doing about the same. She has a testimony, but she is not converted."

How do we differentiate between having a testimony vs. being converted? Elder Dallin H. Oaks offered: "To have a testimony is to know and to feel; to be converted is to do and to become."[1]

Elder Bruce R. McConkie further distinguished between having a testimony and being converted. He stated:

"But this is not all. It is more than believing and knowing. We must be doers of the word and not hearers only. It is more than lip service; it is not simply confessing with the mouth of the divine Sonship of the Savior. It is obedience and conformity and personal righteousness."[2]

To me, what Elders Oaks and McConkie reveal is that it's not enough to simply have a testimony—although a testimony is a prerequisite to conversion. Rather, one must both have a testimony and be converted to the gospel of Jesus Christ in order to be able to stand. Elder James E. Faust taught: "True disciples are those who go beyond simply believing. They act out their belief and follow the Divine Master. Their actions are in harmony with their beliefs."[3]

When we are truly converted and strive to keep the commandments, we protect ourselves against temptation, which is analogous to putting on "the whole armor of God" (see Eph. 6:11).

Become converted unto the Lord

Several years ago, I heard a senior employee in the Church's Missionary Department speak about a study his office was doing about the retention of converts in the Church. The intent of this study was to identify the key factors determining whether a new member would be retained in their membership or would fall into inactivity.

The results of this study were simple and clear: those who were *converted unto the Lord* never did fall away, while those who were converted unto the missionaries, or the members, or the social programs of the Church, were less likely to remain strong.

I was particularly struck by the phrase—"converted unto the Lord"—as if hearing it for the first time. I don't know why it hadn't registered with me before. I had read the *Book of Mormon* many times, but it hadn't stood out to me until it was pointed out in such a meaningful way.

Since becoming aware of this phrase, I've recognized that being "converted unto the Lord" is the key ingredient of discipleship throughout the *Book of Mormon*. I've come to realize that what a person is converted to, and what their faith is in, determines their steadfastness.

Below is a sampling of several scriptures in the *Book of Mormon* that mention the state of the people who were converted unto the Lord:

Alma 19:31: ". . . and as many as heard his words believed and were converted unto the Lord."

Alma 23: 6: ". . . as many of the Lamanites [who were] converted unto the Lord, never did fall away."

Alma 24: 19: ". . . when these Lamanites were brought to believe and to know the truth, they were firm . . ."

Alma 27:27: ". . . for they were distinguished for their zeal towards God; and they were firm in the faith in Christ, even unto the end."

Alma 53:10: ". . . by the power and word of God, they had been converted unto the Lord."

Helaman 15:7-8: ". . . as many of them as are brought to the knowledge of the truth...are firm and steadfast in the faith."

3 Nephi 6:14: ". . . the church was broken up in all the land save it were among a few of the Lamanites who were converted unto the true faith; and they would not depart from it."

3 Nephi 7:21: ". . . and there were but few who were converted unto the Lord; but as many as were converted did truly signify unto the people that they had been visited by the power and Spirit of God, which was in Jesus Christ, in whom they believed."

Elder Dale Renlund explained it this way:

"Being 'converted unto the Lord' means leaving one course of action, directed by an old belief system, and adopting a new one based on faith in Heavenly Father's plan and in Jesus Christ and His Atonement. This change is more than an intellectual acceptance of gospel teachings. It shapes our identity, transforms our understanding of life's meaning, and leads to unchanging fidelity to God. Personal desires that are contrary to being anchored to the Savior and to following the covenant path fade away and are replaced by a determination to submit to the will of Heavenly Father.

"Being converted unto the Lord starts with an unwavering commitment to God, followed by making that commitment part of who we are. Internalizing such a commitment is a lifelong process that requires patience and ongoing repentance. Eventually, this commitment becomes part of who we are, embedded in our sense of self, and ever present in our lives. Just as we never forget our own name no matter what else we are thinking about, we never forget a commitment that is etched in our hearts."[4]

In his final address to his people, King Benjamin

summarized these concepts beautifully: "If you believe all these things [testimony], then see that you do them" [conversion] (Mosiah 4:10).

Be valiant in the testimony of Jesus

My daughter, Hannah, works for a high-tech sales company who hosts an annual conference where they bring in all of their international employees each year. With her company being headquartered in Utah, Hannah fields a myriad of questions about the Church and her membership in it.

This past conference, she was determined to be ready for the questions that would inevitably come her way. Before the conference, she armed herself with several copies of the *Book of Mormon*, pamphlets of the testimony of Joseph Smith, and even copies of the booklet, *For the Strength of Youth*. Because she was prayerful and prepared, Hannah created multiple opportunities to have gospel-centered conversations with her fellow attendees. She did so in a natural, not a forced, way and ended up giving away all of her literature.

One individual from Scandinavia was particularly interested in the Church from a social standpoint. He was a father of two teenagers, and he was genuinely astonished at how it was possible to abide by such lofty standards as a young adult.

Hannah explained that although it may seem counterintuitive, God's commandments are actually freeing rather than restrictive, as they keep us from falling into the binding traps of sin, addiction, and unhappiness. She testified to him of the reality of God, and of her very real knowledge that we are His children. She shared her belief that everything the Lord asks of us is for our good and for our growth and advancement. This fine man was extremely receptive to the Spirit, and Hannah felt prompted to give him the pamphlet, *For the Strength of Youth*, to share with his children, which he willingly accepted.

This instance illustrates how when we open our mouths, and are valiant in the testimony of Jesus, we can be an influence for good in helping to build the kingdom of God upon the earth.

In the 76th Section of the Doctrine and Covenants, Joseph Smith and Sidney Rigdon received a vision of the three degrees of glory. When they saw those individuals who were to inherit the terrestrial world, Joseph referred to one aspect of their state as such: "These are they who are *not* valiant in the testimony of Jesus" (vs. 79).

Can you imagine the regret and disappointment an individual must feel in being described in such a way? President Ezra Taft Benson declared: "Not to be valiant in one's testimony is a tragedy of eternal consequence."[5]

I've spent years seeking clarification as to what it means "to be valiant in the testimony of Jesus." Here are a few descriptions from latter-day Apostles, which I particularly value:

- "'Those who are just and true!' (D&C 76:53) . . . is an apt expression for those valiant in the testimony of Jesus. They are courageous in defending truth and righteousness. These are members of the Church who magnify their callings in the Church (see D&C 84:33), pay their tithes and offerings, live morally clean lives, sustain their

Church leaders by word and action, keep the Sabbath as a holy day, and obey all the commandments of God.[6]

- "To be valiant in the testimony of Jesus is to take the Lord's side on every issue."[7]
- "To be valiant in the testimony of Jesus is to believe in Christ and His gospel with unshakeable conviction. It is to know of the verity and divinity of the Lord's work on earth."[8]
- "The best way to valiantly testify of Jesus is to become steadily more like Him."[9]

In essence, what President Benson and Elders McConkie and Maxwell are characterizing is that to be valiant in the testimony of Jesus, one must view this mortal experience through the lens of the gospel, courageously testify of the reality of God, Jesus Christ and His restored Church, strive to live a Christ-like life—and then, like the Savior, "[go] about doing good" (see Acts 10:38). In the process, we become thoroughly converted unto the Lord and will "never fall away" (see Alma 23:6).

An incident in the life of President Joseph F. Smith is a wonderful example of being true at all times. In the fall of 1857, when 19-year-old Joseph F. was returning from his mission to Hawaii, he joined a wagon train in California. It was a precarious time for Latter-day Saints. Johnston's Army was marching toward Utah, and many had bitter feelings toward the Church.

One evening, several ruffians rode into the wagon train camp, cursing and threatening to hurt every Mormon they could find. Most in the wagon train hid in the brush, but Joseph F. thought to himself: "Shall I run from these fellows? Why should I fear them?"

With that, he walked up to one of the intruders, who, with pistol in hand, demanded, "Are you a 'Mormon'?"

Joseph F. responded, "Yes, siree; dyed in the wool; true blue, through and through."

At that, the thug grasped his hand and said, "Well you are the [expletive-laced] pleasantest man I ever met! Shake, young fellow, I am glad to see a man that stands up for his convictions."[10]

This experience reminds me of a poem I learned in Primary:

Dare to be a Mormon;
Dare to stand alone.
Dare to have a purpose firm;
Dare to make it known.

How crucial it is to remain strong and true, always prepared, and ready to give a reason for the faith that is in us.

It's worth the effort

Former General Young Women president, Sister Bonnie Oscarson, spoke in general conference about the concerted effort we must put forward in order to keep our covenants.

In addition to studying the fundamental doctrines of the gospel and obtaining an unshakable testimony of their truthfulness, she recommended three additional steps we must take that are essential to our conversion:

First, we need to acknowledge the centrality of God our Eternal Father and His Son, Jesus Christ, to our faith and salvation.

Second, we need to understand the need for the

restoration of the doctrine, organization, and keys of authority in these latter days.

And third, we need to study and understand temple ordinances and covenants.[11]

Sister Oscarson noted that it is remarkable to think about what one person of faith and action (a converted woman) can accomplish in this work with the help of the Lord. Indeed, "we shall know them by their fruits" (Matthew 7:16).

At times, honest doubts may arise in our minds and hearts. Yet, when we have a genuine desire to know the truth and exercise our moral agency, these doubts can be resolved. The gospel is a plan of action, and as we obey its principles and ordinances, we will have its truthfulness confirmed to our souls. Remember the promise of the Savior: "If any man will *do* his will, he shall *know* of the doctrine, whether it be of God, or whether I speak of myself" (John 7: 17).

Through the process of authentic struggle, faith ripens into testimony, and our conversion ultimately becomes firmer, stronger, and more substantial.

Be true to the gospel

In a general conference talk entitled "Converted unto the Lord," Elder David A. Bednar spoke on the relationship between receiving a testimony of Jesus Christ and becoming converted to Him and His gospel. He reiterated the concept that testimony alone will not be sufficient to provide the spiritual protection needed to stand in these last days.

To make his case, Elder Bednar likened the relationship of testimony and conversion to the lamps and oil in the Parable of the Ten Virgins. The lamps are to represent testimony and the oil to represent conversion. He further explained:

"As the wise virgins emphasized properly, each of us must 'buy for ourselves.' These inspired women were not describing a business transaction; rather they were emphasizing our individual responsibility to keep our lamp of testimony burning and to obtain an ample supply of the oil of conversion. This precious oil is acquired one drop at a time, 'line upon line (and) precept upon precept' (2 Nephi 28:30). Patiently and persistently."[12]

Ultimately, it is "they that are wise and have received the truth, and have taken the Holy Spirit for their guide," who will resist temptation, avoid deception, and "abide the day" (D&C 45:56-57). As members of the Church, we must not only know that the gospel is true, but accordingly, be true to the gospel.

Before departing on her Church Educational Service (CES) mission with her husband, Bob, to the Alpine/German-Speaking Mission, my friend, Diane Lake, shared the story of her ancestor, Daniel Spencer, in her farewell speech:

"Daniel Spencer was born in West Stockbridge, Massachusetts, on July 20, 1794. Before he turned 21, he had established his character and social position in life. Among his townsmen he was universally respected, and he enjoyed the confidence of the people in the region all around.

"Until 1840, no Elder of the Mormon Church had preached in his native town. Up to this date, Daniel Spencer had no relationship whatever with the people with whom he and his brother Orson afterward became so prominently identified. Daniel Spencer belonged to no sect of religionists but sustained in the community the name of a man marked for character and moral worth. The 'Mormon' Elder came, and his coming created an epoch in Daniel Spencer's life.

"Through Daniel's influence, the Presbyterian meetinghouse was obtained for the 'Mormon' Elder to preach the gospel, and the elite of the town attended the meeting. At the close of the service, the Elder asked the assembly if there was any one present who would give him 'a night's lodging and a meal of victuals in the name of Jesus.' For several minutes, a dead silence reigned in the congregation. None present seemed desirous to peril their character or taint their respectability by taking home a 'Mormon' Elder.

"At length, Daniel Spencer, in the old Puritan spirit and the proud independence so characteristic of the true American gentleman, rose up, stepped into the aisle, and broke the silence: 'I will entertain you, sir, for humanity's sake.' Daniel took the poor Elder, not to his public hotel, as was his wont with the preachers generally who needed hospitality, but he took him to his own house, a fine family mansion, and the next morning, he clothed him from head to foot with a good suit of broad cloth from the shelves of his store.

"The Elder continued to preach the new and strange gospel and brought upon himself much persecution. This produced upon the mind of Daniel Spencer an extra-ordinary effect. Seeing the bitter malevolence from the preachers and the best of the professing Christians, and being naturally a philosopher and a judge, he resolved to investigate the cause of this enmity and unchristian behavior. The result came. It was as strongly marked as his conduct during the investigation.

"For two weeks, Daniel Spencer closed his establishment, refused to do business with anyone, and shut himself up to study, and there alone with his God, he weighed in the balances of his clear head and conscientious heart the divine message, and found it not wanting. One day, when his son was with him in his study, Daniel suddenly burst into a flood of tears, and exclaimed: 'The thing is true, and as an honest man I must embrace it; but it will cost me all I have got on earth.'

"He had weighed the consequences, but his conscientious mind compelled him to assume the responsibility and take up the cross. He saw that he must, in the eyes of friends and townsmen, fall from the social pinnacle on which he then stood to that of a despised people.

"At midday, about three months after the poor 'Mormon' Elder came into the town, Daniel Spencer, having issued a public notice to his townsmen that he should be baptized at noon on a certain day, took the Elder by the arm and, not ashamed, walked through the town taking the route of the main street to the waters of baptism, followed by hundreds of his townsmen to the river's bank.

"The profoundest respect and reverence were manifested by the vast concourse of witnesses, but also the profoundest astonishment. It was nothing wonderful that a despised 'Mormon' Elder should believe in Joseph Smith, but it was a matter of astonishment that a man of Daniel Spencer's social standing and character should accept the mission of the Prophet and the divinity of the *Book of*

Mormon.

"The conversion and conduct of Daniel Spencer carried a deep and weighty conviction among many good families in the region round about, which ultimately resulted in the establishment of a flourishing branch of the Church.

"Daniel went on to serve four missions for the Church. I am so very grateful for the example of this valiant ancestor as a disciple of Jesus Christ and the influence he has had upon his descendants ever since."[13]

This good man gave all he had for the sake of the truth. The integrity shown by Daniel Spencer reminds me that I don't need to look any further than my own heritage to confirm the truth of the query President Gordon B. Hinckley put forth: "It's true, isn't it? Then what else really matters?"[14]

My grandmother on my mother's side, Erika Bienert Merrill, was a convert to the Church from East Berlin, Germany. When the missionaries tracted into her family, Erika's mother and two sisters were receptive to their teachings and began taking the discussions.

Contrary to the interest shown by her mother and sisters, Erika and her father were extremely stubborn and refused to listen to the gospel message. Whenever the missionaries came over, they would hide in the kitchen and make as much noise as possible, banging pots and pans and shuffling furniture around to show their displeasure.

However, after a while, Erika started placing her ear against the door to listen to the message of the restored gospel, and little by little, she began to gain a testimony of its truthfulness. When her mother and sisters committed to be baptized, Erika admitted that she wished to be baptized as well.

In those days, when converts were baptized in Europe, they were asked to gather with the Saints in Salt Lake City. As her family prepared to immigrate to America, her father pled, "Not you too, Erika. Are you going to leave me too?" Erika replied, "I must, Father, for it is true."

Our commitment to God

When studying *Teachings of Presidents of the Church: Howard W. Hunter*, I was particularly touched by the content of the chapter entitled "Our Commitment to God." In this discourse, President Hunter differentiates between making a "contribution" as a member of the Church vs. making a "total commitment." He writes:

"A successful life, the good life, the righteous Christian life requires something more than a contribution, though every contribution is valuable. Ultimately, it requires commitment—whole-souled, deeply held, eternally cherished commitment to the principles we know to be true in the commandments God has given."[15]

Essentially, President Hunter is describing the covenant path Daniel Spencer and Erika Bienert pursued when they became converted to the gospel of Jesus Christ, and the course we all must follow as converted members of the Church.

In recent years, we have witnessed the death of our beloved prophet, Thomas S. Monson, and the ascendency of a new president, Russell M. Nelson, to the highest ranks of the Church.

Elder Gary E. Stevenson of the Quorum of the Twelve

Apostles described the process of calling a new prophet — explaining that upon the last heartbeat of President Monson, the mantle of apostolic leadership passed to President Russell M. Nelson, who is now the senior living Apostle of God on the earth.

Drawing from the words of President Spencer W. Kimball following the death of President David O. McKay, Elder Stevenson affirmed:

"The work of the Lord is endless. Even when a powerful leader dies, not for a single instant is the Church without leadership, thanks to the kind providence who gave his kingdom continuity and perpetuity. As it has already happened . . . [16 times] before in this dispensation, a people reverently close a grave, dry their tears, and turn their faces to the future."[16]

In times of transition, we women of the Church must take our place and exhibit our conversion through both word and deed to the gospel of Jesus Christ. As President Russell M. Nelson reiterates:

"We . . . need your strength, your conversion, your conviction, your ability to lead, your wisdom, and your voices. The kingdom of God is not and cannot be complete without women who make sacred covenants and then keep them, women who can speak with the power and authority of God!"[17]

With all the energy of my heart, I witness the truthfulness of the gospel of Jesus Christ and of His restored Church. In doing so, I acknowledge the divinity of its wellspring. May we strive to be valiant in the testimony of Jesus and truly converted unto the Lord.

Initiatives to consider

1) To have a testimony is to know and to feel; to be converted is to be and to do. Where are you on this continuum?

2) How can you become truly converted and never fall away?

3) Being "converted unto the Lord" is more than believing and knowing. How can you more fully be a "doer" of the word and not a "hearer" only?

---

[1] Dallin H. Oaks, qtd. in Kenneth Johnson, *Contemplations of a Convert* (Deseret Book, 2000), 106.

[2] Bruce R. McConkie, "Be Valiant in the Fight of Faith," *Ensign*, Nov. 1974.

[3] James E. Faust, "Disciple of Christ," *Ensign*, May 1985.

[4] Dale G. Renlund, "Unwavering Commitment to Jesus Christ," General Conference, Oct. 2019.

[5] Ezra T. Benson, "Valiant in the Testimony of Jesus," *Ensign*, Feb. 1987.

[6] *Ibid.*

[7] Bruce R. McConkie, "Be Valiant in the Fight of Faith," *Ensign*, Nov. 1974.

[8] *Ibid.*

[9] Neal A. Maxwell, "Consecrate thy Performance," *Ensign*, May 2002.

[10] Joseph F. Smith, *Teachings of Presidents of the Church: Joseph F. Smith* (The Church of Jesus Christ of Latter-day Saints, 1998), 104.

[11] Bonnie L. Oscarson, "Rise up in Strength, Sisters in Zion," *Ensign*, Nov. 2016.

[12] David A. Bednar, "Converted unto the Lord," *Ensign*, Nov. 2012.

[13] Diane Lake, Missionary Farewell, 30 Apr. 2017.

[14] Gordon B. Hinckley, "It's True, Isn't It?," *Ensign*, July 1993.

[15] Howard W. Hunter, *Teachings of Presidents of the Church: Howard W. Hunter* (The Church of Jesus Christ of Latter-day Saints, 2015), 246.

[16] Gary E. Stevenson, qtd. in Marianne Holman Prescott, "Elder Stevenson Shares Personal Experience in the Calling of a New Prophet," *Church News*, 25 Jan. 2018, www.churchofjesuschrist.org/church/news/elder-stevenson-shares-personal-experience-in-the-calling-of-a-new-prophet.

[17] Russell M. Nelson, "A Plea to My Sisters," *Ensign*, Nov. 2015.

Chapter 3
Mission

I believe in the principle that I can make a difference in
this world.

— President Gordon B. Hinckley

When Dave and I were expecting our third child, we
took a trip to Los Angeles. While there, we saw the
Broadway traveling production of *Phantom of the Opera*.
This was our first time seeing the play, and we were
mesmerized by its hauntingly beautiful music.

The highlight for me came when Raoul sang to
Christine Daae, "Christine, that's all I ask of you." At that
moment, I turned to my husband, and gushed: "I have
never loved a name more. If this child is a girl, we have got
to name her Christine."

A few months later, we gave birth to a baby girl, and
as vowed, we did name her Christine. Many people told us
that she was the most beautiful baby they had ever seen,
and she continues to be a lovely young woman today. With
her permission, I'd like to share her story . . .

Fast-forward nineteen years. We are watching the

41

Saturday morning session of general conference, and President Thomas S. Monson announces the age change for prospective missionaries. Young men are now allowed to serve at age 18, while young women may enter the mission field at age 19.

Christine begins screaming and jumping up and down. "Does this mean I can go on my mission now?"

When we assured her that this was exactly what it meant, she immediately texted our Bishop to ask, "May I please set up an interview with you? I want to go on a mission as soon as possible!"

Since she was a little girl, Christine was instilled with a desire to serve a fulltime mission. There was never a question in her mind that this is what she wanted to do. She considered eighteen months of her life to be a small sacrifice for the gospel she loved so much. To think that she could go out two years earlier than planned was a dream come true!

Christine submitted her mission papers in record time, and within twenty-three days of the prophet's announcement, she received her call to serve in the California Los Angeles Mission. Half of her time was to be spent in the Los Angeles Temple Visitor's Center, and the other half spent proselyting. It was a perfect call for her, and she couldn't have been happier.

She was one of the first nineteen-year-old sister missionaries to receive her endowment in the Bountiful Temple, and one of the first to enter the Provo MTC. She thrived during her weeks at the MTC, and she began immersing herself in the work of the Lord. There could not have been a more desirous or prepared missionary than Christine.

After arriving in Los Angeles, she was assigned to a companion and began participating fully in mission life. Up at 6:30 a.m. to exercise and take part in personal and companion study, then out to proselyte or to the Visitor's Center—rotating schedules daily.

However, within a week, Christine began experiencing a downheartedness that inexplicably came over her. She felt a deep sadness—almost a despondency—so tangible that it became paralyzing. Some of the time she was able to shake it off, but increasingly, it began to take over her very presence, making it impossible for her to teach—and at times, to even talk.

Her companion began having to trade off with other sisters because they had an appointment to teach an investigator and Christine was unable to move; during those times, the other sister who was left behind would stay with Christine while she sat trancelike, curled up in a corner of the room.

The one source of solace Christine received was when she was in the Los Angeles Temple Visitor's Center standing next to the Christus. When she listened to the recorded words of the Lord playing for the visitors, she felt a sense of contentment—"the peace of God, which passeth all understanding" (Phil. 4:7), and she knew that she was known of and loved by the Lord.

Five weeks after arriving in the mission field, the Missionary Committee in Salt Lake City determined that, in the best interest of her emotional well-being, Christine should return home. Although this decision dashed her lifelong dream of serving a mission, she carried within her the spiritual confirmation that she had given everything she had, and the Lord was pleased with her whole-souled offering. "For I, the Lord, will judge all men according to their works, according to the desire of their hearts" (D&C 137:9).

When our inspired stake president honorably released Christine, he assured her (and us) that she had truly given her all and that her offering was acceptable to our Heavenly Father. With her heart breaking, but with every ounce of courage she could muster, Christine faithfully testified: "I know God has a plan for me."

Upon her return, Christine was referred to the Church's Missionary Clinic, where she was diagnosed with depression and anxiety. She began working with a remarkable, and very empathetic, counselor who helped her regain a sense of normalcy and wellness, despite many struggles along the way.

Within two months, she was back in school, and within a year, Christine met Josh, a worthy and faithful priesthood holder. They were married in the Salt Lake Temple exactly a year-and-a-half after her early return from her mission. She often wonders if she would have missed the opportunity to meet and marry her husband had she remained on her mission.

Now a woman in her late twenties, Christine is beautiful in every way. Although she continues to battle these emotional challenges, with medical help and therapy, she manages her depression and anxiety well. Her testimony that God does indeed have a plan for her is what has sustained her through the difficult experience of having to cut her mission short. Having faith in this plan has made all the difference in the world and gives meaning and purpose to her life.

In his book, *When All You've Ever Wanted Isn't*

Enough: The Search for a Life that Matters, Rabbi Harold Kushner reiterates this principle. He writes: "Our souls are not hungry for fame, comfort, wealth, or power. Our souls are hungry for meaning, for the sense that we have figured out how to live so that our lives matter, so that the world will be at least a little bit different for our having passed through it."[1]

Missions are to be 'detected,' not 'invented'

I have believed since I was very young that every life has a purpose. My father used to teach us children: "We don't *invent* our missions, we *detect* them."[2] Dad further explained that our personal life mission is revealed to us through the whisperings and guidance of the Holy Spirit, rather than through the determination of our own desires or interests.

In January 2017, Wendy Watson Nelson (wife of President Russell M. Nelson) gave the keynote speech at our stake women's conference. She shared her sincere belief that while in the preexistence, each of us made promises of things we would do and the people we would become during our mortal existence.

Sister Nelson wistfully expressed the desire for a premortal DVD player that would allow us to rewind our mortal lives and glance back into our premortal state. She insisted that if we could only remember these premortal promises, our entire perspective would change as to the concept of who we really are and what we have covenanted to do "whilst in this tabernacle of clay" (see Moroni 9:6).

President Spencer W. Kimball taught a similar

doctrine to the sisters of the Relief Society: "Before we came [to earth, we] were given certain assignments . . .While we do not now remember the particulars, this does not alter the glorious reality of what we once agreed to."[3]

"What we once agreed to" is to follow divine light and inspiration in the pursuit of our divine missions; to humbly allow God to "lead [us] by the hand and give [us] answer to [our] prayers" (D&C 112:10). Along the way, we must recognize that if we are good at some things, or can become good at them, this is most likely an indication of our life's work and purpose. Our aim is to "detect, not invent" our own personal mission, and then to pursue it with all the energy of our hearts.

As James Hillman puts it: "Your life's work is to find your life's work—and then to exercise the discipline, tenacity, and hard work it takes to pursue it."[4]

The role and influence of righteous women

In her inaugural address to the sisters in the General Women's Meeting, Sister Sharon Eubank, first counselor in the general presidency of the Relief Society, boldly charged:

"The prophets are calling on us, my sisters. Will you be righteous? Will you articulate your faith? Can you bear being distinct and different? Will your happiness in spite of your trials draw others who are good and noble and who need your friendship? Will you turn on your light? I testify the Lord Jesus Christ will go before us and be in our midst."[5]

To me, hers is a plea to find our voices, to detect our personal life missions, and to discover how the gifts and talents God has blessed us with may go hand-in-hand with and bolster the growth and development of the kingdom of God upon the earth. As we lend our talents to His magnificent work, He will use us in remarkable ways to bless those around us and bring about His purposes.

As Latter-day Saint sisters, Sister Eubank specifies in particular that we must become better at articulating the reasons for our faith. My friend, Si Foster, is an excellent example of a person who does just this.

Si writes a popular food blog and maintains an Instagram account (*A Bountiful Kitchen*), where she is constantly sharing spiritual thoughts and examples of how she is blessed by the Lord and His Church. Her greatest desire is to use her voice for good in sharing not only helpful recipes and hints for the home cook, but the basis of her testimony.

For instance, on Valentine's Day, Si posted a photo of herself and her husband in front of the Salt Lake Temple with the following sentiment: "The sweetest place to celebrate Valentine's Day."[6]

On Easter, she posted a photo of her little granddaughter next to the Christus on Temple Square, with the caption: "I stand all amazed at the love Jesus offers me . . . I'm grateful to know, without a doubt, that He lives and loves us!"[7]

After attending a "life-changing" evening session of stake conference, Si posted this beautiful expression: "During the meeting, Elder Gifford Nielson asked us what our favorite scripture is in the *Book of Mormon*. He asked us to share that scripture with someone we love and tell them why and have them do the same. For the past five years, I have read the *Book of Mormon* cover to cover. I don't tell you this to boast, but only to say that reading the *Book of Mormon* consistently has changed my life."[8]

Si Foster (*A Bountiful Kitchen*), Si's daughter, Corrine Stokoe (*Mint Arrow*), Stephanie Nielsen (*NieNieDialogues*), Rhonna Farrer (*rhonnafarrer*), Lizzy Jensen (*The Small Seed*), and many others are just a sampling of some of the LDS women who write popular blogs with thousands, and in some cases, millions, of followers. Each of these sisters has found a vehicle to share her voice. The women who read their words are drawn to their faith, their passion, and their certitude, and they are not left to wonder why they are different.

Rather, these converted Latter-day Saint women "are not ashamed of the gospel of Christ" (Romans 1:16), and "[are] ready always to give an answer to every man that asketh [them] a reason of the hope that is in [them]" (1 Peter 3:15). Regardless of their topic, whether it be motherhood, food, or fashion, they speak with the power of a converted woman's voice, and impact for good many within their sphere of influence.

In regard to the effect of Latter-day Saint women on the good women of the world prior to the Second Coming of the Savior, President Spencer W. Kimball made a remarkable prophecy to the women of the Church nearly 40 years ago. Towards the conclusion of his speech, he encouraged:

"Finally, my dear sisters, may I suggest to you something that has not been said before or at least in quite this way. Much of the major growth that is coming to the Church in the last days will come because many of the good women of the world . . . will be drawn to the Church in large numbers. This will happen to the degree that the women of the Church reflect righteousness and articulateness in their lives and to the degree that the women of the Church are seen as distinct and different— in happy ways—from the women of the world. . . It will be . . . female exemplars of the Church [who] will be a significant force in both the numerical and the spiritual growth of the Church in the last days."[9]

In our era, Elder Russell M. Nelson has appealed to the sisters in a similar manner:

"I plead with my sisters of The Church of Jesus Christ of Latter-day Saints to step forward! Take your rightful and needful place in your home, in your community, and in the kingdom of God—more than you ever have before. I plead with you to fulfill President Kimball's prophecy. And I promise you in the name of Jesus Christ that as you do so, the Holy Ghost will magnify your influence in an unprecedented way!"[10]

Our greatest fulfillment

President Gordon B. Hinckley said: 'Women for the most part see their greatest fulfillment, their greatest happiness, in home and family. God planted within women something divine that expresses itself in quiet strength, in refinement, in peace, in goodness, in virtue, in truth, in love. *And all of these remarkable qualities find their truest and most satisfying expression in motherhood.*'

He continued: 'The greatest job that any woman will ever do will be in nurturing and teaching and living and encouraging and rearing her children in righteousness and truth. There is no other thing that will compare with that, regardless of what she does."[11]

Not long before passing away, President Joseph F. Smith received a Vision of the Redemption of the Dead, where he was able to see into the Spirit World. He observed many of the noble and great ones who were chosen in the beginning to be rulers in the Church of God. Among those he saw, who were assembled in this vast congregation of the righteous, were Father Adam, and our "glorious Mother Eve" (D&C 138:39).

That descriptive phrase, "our glorious Mother Eve," has always struck me and reminded me of my mother. Like Eve, my mother Sandra was a faithful daughter who worshiped the true and living God.

Mom was such a loving and nurturing mother, and so much fun to boot! On one occasion, my sisters and I asked Mom what she regretted as a mother when looking back on her life. At the time, all five of us daughters were stretched to the limits by the demands of raising small children, and we felt somewhat guilt-ridden and overwhelmed. Mom paused for a moment to consider our question, and then she responded: "Hmm . . . Well, I probably would have celebrated Memorial Day better." What? We were astounded! That was it? After raising nine children? To better celebrate Memorial Day? How could she possibly have no regrets?

Later on, Mom explained the secret to her contentment: "Well, I certainly made my share of mistakes; I didn't do everything right. But I can honestly say that I did the very best I could. I literally poured myself into each one of you, and I gave my family all that I had—my whole heart and soul."

Even in her last few years, Mom would frequently ask:

"What can I do to be a better matriarch within our family? How can I specifically help you and your children?" She recognized that she was living on borrowed time, and she felt a sense of urgency about making a difference within her circle of influence. She was continually striving to improve and to be a better individual, mother, grandmother, sister, friend, and Church member. She cheerfully did all things that lay within her power (see D&C 123:17). How grateful I am for her beautiful example!

President Russell M. Nelson shared a very tender experience while speaking to the sisters of the Church in the General Women's meeting. He said:

"One day while I was speaking to a congregation in South America, I became exceedingly excited about my topic, and at a pivotal moment, I said, 'As the *mother* of 10 children, I can tell you that. . .' And then I went on to complete my message.

"I did not realize that I had said the word *mother.* My translator, assuming I had misspoken, changed the word *mother* to *father,* so the congregation never knew that I had referred to myself as *mother.* But my wife Wendy heard it, and she was delighted with my Freudian slip.

"In that moment, the deep longing of my heart to make a difference in the world—like only a mother does—bubbled up from my heart. Through the years, whenever I have been asked why I *chose* to become a medical doctor, my answer has always been the same: 'Because I could not *choose* to be a mother.'

"Please note that anytime I use the word *mother,* I am not talking only about women who have given birth or adopted children in this life. I am speaking about *all* of our

Heavenly Parents' adult daughters. Every woman is a mother by virtue of her eternal divine destiny.

"So tonight, as the *father* of 10 children—*nine daughters* and one son—and as President of the Church, I pray that you will sense how deeply I feel about you—about who you are and all the good you can do. No one can do what a righteous woman can do. No one can duplicate the influence of a mother."[12]

I could not agree more. I would like to pay tribute to *my glorious mother Sandra* who, among countless other things, has taught me to fill the world with love, to live life with no regrets, and to waste and wear out my life in the pursuit of truth and righteousness. I am so grateful for her love, her light, her goodness, and her modeling of what it means to be a righteous mother.

God honors the personal missions of His children

All of us need a vision for our lives. I am incredibly inspired by those who have found their voice and passion through discovering their unique personal missions. I believe God honors the personal missions of His children because it's not about them—it's about serving His other children in ways that are unique to that individual.

On December 3, 2016, my husband Dave and I drove to Alpine, Utah, for an open house for *Bridle Up Hope: The Rachel Covey Foundation*. We had no clue as to the impact this visit would have upon us, and we were literally blown away by what we saw and felt.

Our 21-year-old niece, Rachel, had passed away in September 2012, after which her parents, Rebecca and Sean Covey, struggled to find purpose and meaning. That is until they established *Bridle Up Hope: The Rachel Covey Foundation* in January 2013. Its mission is to inspire hope and confidence through equestrian training—an activity for which Rachel was passionate. The program is specifically designed for young women, ages 12-25, who may be wrestling with depression or anxiety, or have experienced trauma or abuse, or have simply lost hope in life.

The moment we walked into the restored farmhouse with my father's 'Seven Habits' painted on the walls, we could feel his and Rachel's presence. I became very emotional and couldn't hold back the tears. There was no doubt that the Spirit of the Lord was there in abundance.

The purpose of the open house was to introduce a new location, a refurbished farmhouse, landscaped pastures, and a riding arena—all contained within sturdy fencing surrounding the property, which consists of 130 prime acres nestled snugly into the foothills. Many sacred miracles led up to Sean and Rebecca obtaining this property; suffice it to say, heaven was instrumental in making it happen!

It's remarkable how something so beautiful can emerge from something so tragic—Isaiah calls this phenomenon "beauty for ashes." He prophesies: "To appoint unto them that mourn in Zion, to give unto them beauty for ashes, the oil of joy for mourning, the garment of praise for the spirit of heaviness; that they might be called trees of righteousness, the planting of the LORD, that he might be glorified"(Isaiah 61:3).

I firmly believe that miracles continue to take place within this organization because *Bridle Up Hope* is making such a positive difference in the lives of so many young women. God is mindful of His daughters, and He is particularly aware of those who struggle with depression, anxiety, and issues of self-worth. Besides . . . there is something magical that happens between a girl and her horse.[13]

We are all aware of those who, like Sean and Rebecca, are infused with a sense of mission and who go to great lengths to accomplish what they are driven to do. I, too, have such a friend named Nikki Eberhardt.

Since she was a young girl, Nikki has been compelled by a sense of mission to give voice to the disenfranchised and to provide a space for them to become empowered. She defines herself as a 'global citizen,' and she has worked passionately to tackle the world's greatest challenges through innovative social enterprise.

Nikki has confronted tough issues such as helping to relieve suffering for refugees, alleviating extreme poverty, empowering girls in developing countries (who have limited power) while reinforcing human values, and creating social impact companies, both at home and abroad. Her personal motto is to fulfill Gandhi's charge: "You must be the change you wish to see in the world."

Along the way, Nikki has amassed a litany of prestigious accomplishments, which has helped establish her credibility and influence. During the past several years alone, Nikki has earned degrees from the University of Utah (PhD ABD in Global Sociology), Oxford University (MBA) and Brigham Young University (MA International Development), presented at TED x Oxford 2017, served in leadership roles for the International Refugee Committee, United Way, UN Women, and helped with Global Citizen Festivals—annual advocacy platforms and fundraisers at

Central Park to end extreme poverty—along with a myriad of other initiatives.

Nikki has taught me what it means to be deeply spiritual and yet committed socially. She explains why she is so passionate about her life's mission:

"[I see] this gorgeous face etched into my heart. I crouch next to this tiny Guatemalan, indigenous woman, and reflect. I see poverty and neglect in every place I visit on the globe. I cry tears when I meet beautiful souls trapped in limited bodies born into a system that lacks mobility.

"Life is not fair—there is no reason I won the lottery in terms of ability to learn and experience and choose. This woman is as valuable as I am. She has desires and needs—and is as entitled to happiness as I am. God loves her as He loves me.

"I recommit with laser-sharp focus to succor and empower these souls. I will continue to work to change the system. This is expected of me, and I will with urgency [respond]. God help me."[14]

If we are willing, God will use us. When our hearts and desires are turned to Him and we access His strength, He will magnify our actions to fulfill His righteous purposes.

Embrace your own personal mission

Each of us has a distinct mission inside him or her—one that has the capacity to inspire. Our mission need not be massive or global in scope; the individuals I've referred to above have life missions that are unique to their situations. Rather, our foremost objective should be to impact for good all those within our sphere of influence, however large or small that sphere might be.

Former General Young Women President, Sister Bonnie Oscarson, shared a story that is illustrative of this principle. During a recent general conference address, she told about the experience of a stake Relief Society president who, on a widespread scale, collected quilts for people in need during the 1990s.

She and her daughter drove a truck filled with these quilts from London to Kosovo. On her journey home, she received an unmistakable spiritual impression that sank deep into her heart. The impression was this: "What you have done is a very good thing. Now go home, walk across the street, and serve your neighbor!"

Sister Oscarson went on to caution: "What good does it do to save the world if we neglect the needs of those closest to us and those whom we love the most? How much value is there in fixing the world if the people around us are falling apart and we don't notice? Heavenly Father may have placed those who need us closest to us, knowing that we are best suited to meet their needs."[15]

There is much good that can be done within our own families and in our own neighborhoods and communities. The response to the question of how and where God would have us serve is found in whichever way we are impressed to use our time and talents and to embrace our own personal mission. It all begins with desire.

In latter-day revelation, the Lord reminds: ". . . if you desire, you shall be the means of doing much good in this generation" (D&C 11:8).

I testify that, as my daughter Christine learned, God does indeed have a plan for our lives. If only we could envision our premortal self and realize the divine potential within us, we would rise up and never be the same again. Our loving and eternal Heavenly Father knows who we are and who we are capable of becoming, and He will help us fulfill that destiny.

Initiatives to consider

1) God has an important work for each of us. What is Heavenly Father's plan for you? What specific things has He prepared you to accomplish?

2) What are the gifts, talents, and abilities with which God has blessed you? How can you take who you are, who you want to be, and what you can do, and use it for a purpose greater than yourself?

3) How can you rise up to become the woman of faith and courage Heavenly Father intended you to be?

---

[1] Harold Kushner, *When All You've Ever Wanted Isn't Enough: The Search for a Life that Matters* (Fireside, 1986), 18.

[2] Stephen R. Covey, qtd. in Hyrum Smith, *What Matters Most: The Power of Living Your Values* (Fireside, 2000), 111.

[3] Spencer W. Kimball, "The Role of Righteous Women," *Ensign,* Nov. 1979.

[4] James Hillman, qtd. in Sean Covey, *The 6 Most Important Decisions You'll Ever Make: A Guide for Teens* (Fireside, 2006), 84.

[5] Sharon Eubank, "Turn on Your Light," *Ensign*, Nov. 2017.

[6] Si Foster (A Bountiful Kitchen), *Instagram*, 14 Feb. 2017.

[7] *Ibid*, 16 Apr. 2017.

[8] *Ibid*, 11 Mar. 2018.

[9] Spencer W. Kimball, "The Role of Righteous Women," *Ensign*, Nov. 1979.

[10] Russell M. Nelson, "A Plea to My Sisters," *Ensign,* Nov. 2015.

[11] Gordon B. Hinckley, *Teachings of Gordon B. Hinckley* (Deseret Book, 1997), 387, 390.

[12] Russell M. Nelson, "Sisters' Participation in the Gathering of Israel," *Ensign*, Nov. 2018.

[13] For more information, or to sponsor a girl, please visit *bridleuphope.org.*

[14] Nikki Eberhardt, *Instagram*, 31 Aug. 2015.

[15] Bonnie L. Oscarson, "The Needs Before Us," *Ensign*, Nov. 2017.

Chapter 4
Contentment

Within what is allotted to us, we can have spiritual contentment.

— *Elder Neal A. Maxwell*

As the second oldest of nine children, I loved growing up in a large family. Being surrounded by multiple siblings with whom I could play or talk always made life interesting and exciting. I determined that when I became a mother, I would replicate our family culture.

One of the lessons you learn as you grow older, however, is that there are certain situations over which you have little—to no—control. The timing of when you marry, the number of children you are blessed to have, and the trials that await you are a few of these life circumstances.

My husband Dave and I met and married when he was 28 and I was 26 years old. We started our family right away, and we were blessed to have three children within a four-and-a-half-year period. Then came a five-year span when we were unable to get pregnant.

For the first time in my marriage, I became a "knowing participant" in the struggles of infertility. I experienced the sting when well-meaning family members asked if we were planning on having more children, the humiliation when an insensitive friend called me a "wimp" for "only having three children," and the disappointment of discovering month after month that we were not expecting.

It was during this time that I ran into my second cousin, Irene. We had grown up together on the beach at Hebgen Lake, Montana, and as part of our conversations, we both expressed the yearning desire to raise a large family, similar to the ones we had been raised in.

When Irene asked me about my family, I told her that we had three children, but we wanted more. I expressed unhappiness and discontentment with my present situation rather than being grateful for the children with whom we had been blessed.

In response, Irene told me that they had been unable to have any children at all, despite extensive infertility treatments over a ten-year period. She bore testimony that regardless of her current situation, she knew God was mindful of her and that He had a plan for her life.

The spirit with which she spoke, and her humble submission to the will of the Lord, put me to shame. I felt chastised by the Spirit, and Alma's self-rebuke was brought to the forefront of my mind: "But behold, I am a man, and do sin in my wish; for I ought to be content with the things which the Lord hath allotted me" (Alma 29:3).

God did indeed have a plan for Irene's life. Through some miraculous circumstances, Irene and her husband Paul were eventually able to adopt eight children, and they have raised them in righteousness.

Dave and I were also blessed, eventually, with two more children: Colin Kamakana (meaning "gift from God" in Hawaiian), and Megan Kapi'olani (named after Queen Kapi'olani and the hospital in Honolulu where Megan was born). Our gratitude for these two additional children was intensified due to our initial pain and longing. Truly, "the depth of our understanding was the depth of our gratitude" (President Spencer W. Kimball).

Be content with what the Lord has allotted us

One of the most defining challenges of mortality is learning to be content with the things which the Lord has allotted us. Making peace with our circumstances, particularly when they are not ideal is the core of this state of being. The Apostle Paul expressed this concept to the Philippians: "Not that I speak in respect of want: for I have learned, in whatsoever state I am, therewith to be content" (Phil. 4:11).

President Russell M. Nelson explains:

"My dear brothers and sisters, the joy we feel has little to do with the circumstances of our lives and everything to do with the focus of our lives.

"When the focus of our lives is on God's plan of salvation . . . and Jesus Christ and His gospel, we can feel joy regardless of what is happening—or not happening—in our lives. Joy comes from and because of Him. He is the source of all joy.

"Just as the Savior offers peace that 'passeth all understanding' (Phil. 4:7), He also offers an intensity, depth, and breadth of joy that defy human logic or mortal comprehension. For example, it doesn't seem possible to feel joy when your child suffers with an incurable illness or when you lose your job or when your spouse betrays you. Yet that is precisely the joy the Savior offers. His joy is constant, assuring us that our 'afflictions shall be but a small moment' (D&C 121:7), and be consecrated to our gain (see 2 Nephi 2:2)."[1]

I love the concept that our joy, or contentment, should have little to do with the "circumstances" of our lives, and everything to do with the "focus" of our lives. Said another way, "If our lives and our faith are centered upon Jesus Christ and His restored gospel, nothing can ever go permanently wrong."[2]

Hardships are a necessary part of life; they are inevitable. Our Heavenly Father allows us to experience such difficulties because He wants to refine and hallow us, to develop our character and compassion—to help us become like Him. Even God and Jesus Christ have become who they are because of what they have experienced and overcome.

Attitude is everything

During Fall Break several years ago, my husband Dave and I took a trip to Maui with my siblings and their spouses. We stayed in a condo on Ka'anapali Beach and thoroughly enjoyed our proximity to the ocean, other resorts, and good shopping.

While there, we created the habit of walking each morning along the boardwalk that ran parallel to the beach. Every day, we would come across a bald, older gentleman returning from his morning run. With time, we realized that this was the renowned self-help author and motivational speaker, Wayne Dyer, who was a permanent resident of our building.

One morning, we took the opportunity to introduce ourselves and become acquainted with him. Wayne could not have been more gracious and kind. As a matter of fact, within an hour of meeting him, he had a bellman deliver a personalized copy of one of his books to our room.

Of course, I was familiar with Wayne's prominence in the field of self-development, but I was unacquainted with his content. As I began reading some of his work however, I was impressed with how closely his philosophies corresponded with mine. From Wayne's writings, I've gained more insight into what it means to be content:

1) Look for and acknowledge the hand of God in your life. "With everything that has happened to you, you can either feel sorry for yourself, or treat what has happened as a gift. Everything is either an opportunity to grow or an obstacle to keep you from growing. You get to choose."[3]

2) The way you view your present situation is a precursor to the way you will approach future opportunities. Aesop's adage applies here: "He that is discontented in one place will seldom be content in another."

To illustrate this principle, Wayne tells of an interaction he had with a couple who were visiting Hawaii, and how they revealed to him their plans to move there. When they asked him how he liked living in the islands, Wayne turned the conversation around and asked them his own set of questions.

"Where are you from?" Wayne asked the couple.

"We're from Chicago," answered the couple.

"How do you like living there?" Wayne followed up.

"We don't like it at all," the couple answered. "It's bitter cold, the people are extremely unfriendly, and it's very difficult to navigate."

"Well, then," responded Wayne. "I don't think you'll like living in Hawaii either."

Wayne then proceeds to tell of an experience he had with another couple he met who expressed a similar intent.

"We are planning on moving to Hawaii," they said. "How do you like it here?"

Again, Wayne turned the tables and asked them his own questions.

When he found out that the couple was from New York and that they really liked living there, he assured them that they would really enjoy living in Hawaii as well.

Dr. Dyer summed up this experience by quipping: "Attitude is everything—so pick a good one!"[4]

Approximately nine months after meeting Wayne Dyer in Maui, we learned that he had died of a heart attack at the age of 75. Although he had been diagnosed with cancer a few years before, an autopsy indicated that his body was completely cancer-free when he passed away. His family attributes this to the healing power of his spirit and his abundant positive energy.[5]

While we may not be able to change the circumstances of our lives, we can choose our response to them. President Thomas S. Monson offers this perspective: "We can't direct the wind, but we can adjust the sails. For maximum happiness, peace, and contentment, may we choose a positive attitude."[6]

It's called the plan of happiness

My father-in-law has adopted a life motto that typifies his personality: "Be of good cheer" (D&C 61:36). In every card he writes, in every piece of advice he dispenses, and in every exchange we have with him, he reminds us of this invitation from the Savior. Though life may be filled with challenges, he instructs, with faith we can rise above them. As President Monson used to say: "Be of good cheer. The future is as bright as your faith."[7]

I was reading in the *Deseret News* recently about the tragic death of a 21-year-old Latter-day Saint missionary who was struck and killed in Samoa while walking down a road with his companion. Examining the circumstances more closely, I learned that this missionary, Elder Aaron Ahkau Matapa Patiole, was from Australia, and one of his defining characteristics was his cheerfulness, best personified by his infectious smile.

In a letter to his family, a former companion, Elder Richards, told about the wisdom he had gained from Elder Patiole when they had served together. He wrote:

"I learned a thing or two from my companion, Elder Patiole, this week. So, 24 hours a day, 7 days a week, Elder Patiole is smiling. I always thought that was great and all, but it wasn't until this week that I understood why.

"Up until this point, my previous companions and I have visited many people with no luck or success. Many of the people just went into the books as 'not interested.' But this week when we visited them, they smiled and accepted our message.

"At first, I didn't understand because nothing was different in our teaching, yet they accepted [our message] with a smile. I came to learn this smile was just a reflection of my companion's big[ger] smile.

"After the lesson was over, I talked to my companion about what had just happened, and he gave me these great words of wisdom. "Elder Richards, it is called the plan of HAPPINESS.""

"I am so grateful for each of my companions and all they teach me. This week I learned to put the "happy" in happiness."[8]

What a beautiful example this missionary was, and even in his death, he continues to inspire! How often have I failed to reflect the joy found in God's plan of happiness? The words of Robert Louis Stevenson caution, "For to miss the joy is to miss all!"

Cultivate an attitude of gratitude

For many years, I have kept a list of quotations about what it means to be content. One of the favorite expressions I have come across is one attributed to actress Edie Falco. She said: "My idea of happiness is different now from what it used to be. It's not the jumping-up-and-down kind. It's a contentedness. And the overriding feeling is gratitude."[9]

To my understanding, discontentment and gratitude cannot coexist, since discontentment blocks the perception and experience of life as a gift—just as faith and fear cannot exist in the same person at the same time.

Recognizing God's hand in all things and expressing gratitude for His goodness and mercy can make a positive difference in our outlook on life, and it can literally serve as an antidote for mild depression as it helps us overcome self-pity, selfishness, and loneliness.

Within the past few decades, "well-being" has taken the place of "happiness" as the ideal psychological state to achieve. With the birth of positive psychology, Dr. Martin Seligman, widely considered to be the "father" of this discipline, has identified five measurable elements that contribute to a person's well-being. A useful acronym (PERMA) helps us remember these characteristics:

- Positive emotion: happiness and life satisfaction are aspects of this
- Engagement, interest
- Relationships
- Meaning, purpose
- Achievement

Dr. Seligman notes that engaging in exercises that evoke a sense of gratitude is essential to creating well-being. He writes:

"Gratitude can make your life happier and more satisfying. When we feel gratitude, we benefit from the pleasant memory of a positive event in our life. Also, when we express gratitude to others, we strengthen our relationship with them . . .

"Express your gratitude in a thoughtful, purposeful manner . . .

"You will be happier and less depressed one month from now."[10]

In a landmark article in the *Ensign*, Dr. Vaughn E. Worthen, clinical professor and psychologist at Brigham Young University, corroborates these findings:

"Gratitude is receiving significant attention in the emerging field of positive psychology. As a licensed psychologist, I have extensively researched the use of gratitude interventions in promoting well-being. I find that introducing these interventions into counseling at appropriate times is helpful in treating depression, reducing anxiety, and introducing a more positive focus to troubled relationships.

"Experiencing and expressing gratitude can help all of us—whatever our situation—lead fuller, richer lives."[11]

In essence, what these psychologists have concluded is that although life may not be perfect or free from struggle, experiencing and expressing gratitude can lead to an overall sense of well-being. Knowing that God is mindful of us and being grateful for His abundant blessings is vital to attaining contentment.

President Henry B. Eyring is an excellent example of someone who has created a pattern in his life for identifying his blessings and expressing gratitude. In a general conference talk, he talked about the discipline of writing in a daily journal:

"I wrote down a few lines every day for years. Before I would write, I would ponder this question: 'Have I seen the hand of God reaching out to touch us or our children or our family today?' As I kept at it, something began to happen . . . More than gratitude began to grow in my heart. Testimony grew."[12]

As President Eyring recognized, when we acknowledge God's hand in our lives, our gratitude grows. He then blesses us with increased faith, and even heightened knowledge and testimony.

Many years ago, in my *Excellent Women Book Club,* we read and discussed a book that has had a profound effect upon my understanding of the role gratitude should play in our lives. In *The Return of the Prodigal Son,* Christian writer, Henri L. M. Nouwen, writes:

"Gratitude, however, goes beyond the 'mine' and 'thine' and claims the truth that all of life is a pure gift . . . The discipline of gratitude is the explicit effort to acknowledge that all I am and have is given to me as a gift of love, a gift to be celebrated with joy.

"The choice for gratitude rarely comes without some real effort. But each time I make it, the next choice is a little easier, a little freer, and a little less self-conscious. Because every gift I acknowledge reveals another and another until, finally, even the most normal, obvious, and seemingly mundane event or encounter proves to be filled with grace.

"There is an Estonian proverb that says: 'Who does not thank for little will not thank for much.' Acts of gratitude make one grateful because, step by step, they reveal that all is grace."[13]

I love the concept that gratitude is both a discipline and a choice, and as we deliberately discipline ourselves to make that choice, we begin to see life as a gift to be celebrated with joy.

Recognize the difference between contentment and complacency

When I wrote my first book, *Contentment*, I experienced a bit of pushback from individuals who didn't understand the difference between contentment and complacency. Some people felt that if one were to be content with the status quo, there would be no impetus for change or growth.

I have found that there is a difference between being

content with the things which the Lord hath allotted to us versus ignoring authentic spiritual nudges from the Holy Ghost to improve our lives. Being content does not mean being complacent or satisfied with mediocrity. Rather, it is more an attitude that God is pleased with the direction we are headed, while acknowledging that He can make a lot more out of our lives than we can.

Elder Neal A. Maxwell put it this way: "It is left to each of us to balance contentment regarding what God has allotted to us in life with some divine discontent resulting from what we are in comparison to what we have the power to become."[14]

We may receive the spiritual knowledge that we are headed the right way and are on the path of discipleship, "notwithstanding [our] weakness" (2 Nephi 33:11).

Elder David A. Bednar concurs:

"Following the Savior also enables us to receive 'an actual knowledge that the course of life [we are] pursuing' is in accordance with God's will. Such knowledge is not an unknowable mystery and is not focused primarily upon our temporal pursuits or ordinary mortal concerns. Rather, steady and sustained progress along the covenant pathway is the course of life that is pleasing to Him."[15]

Isaiah taught: "Thou wilt keep him in perfect peace, whose mind is stayed on thee: because he trusteth in thee" (26:3).

What a blessing to understand that though imperfect, we may still please God, and find a measure of contentment through the twists and turns of life as we stay our minds on Him, earn His trust, and remain on the covenant path.

Initiatives to consider

1. How can you learn to be content with the things which the Lord has allotted you even when your circumstances are not ideal?
2. What practices can you engage in to cultivate an attitude of gratitude?
3. Identify the difference between being content with your present situation versus ignoring authentic spiritual nudges from the Holy Ghost to improve your life.

---

[1] Russell M. Nelson, "Joy and Spiritual Survival," *Ensign*, Nov. 2016.
[2] Howard W. Hunter, "'Fear Not, Little Flock,'" *1988–89 Devotional and Fireside Speeches* (Brigham Young University Press, 1989), 112.
[3] Wayne W. Dyer, qtd. in Matt Mayberry, "Remembering Wayne Dyer: 20 Inspirational Quotes to Help You Become a Better You," *Entrepreneur,* 1 Sept. 2015, www.entrepreneur.com/article/250142.
[4] "Dr. Wayne Dyer: Attitude is everything—so pick a good one!," *YouTube*, uploaded by Spiritual Cinema Circle, 1 Jul. 2013, www.youtube.com/watch?v=SCdZWvB_5dM.
[5] Greg Toppo, "Self-help Guru Wayne W. Dyer Dies at 75," *USA TODAY,* 30 Aug. 2015, www.usatoday.com/story/life/people/2015/08/30/wayne-dyer-obituary/71435806.
[6] Thomas S. Monson, "Living the Abundant Life," *Ensign,* Jan. 2012.
[7] Thomas S. Monson, "Be of Good Cheer," *Ensign*, May 2009.
[8] *Deseret News*, 20 Nov. 2017.
[9] *Woman's World*, Sept. 28, 2009.
[10] Martin Seligman, *Flourish: A Visionary New Understanding of Happiness and Well-Being* (Atria, 2011), 24, 30-31)

[11] Vaughn E. Worthen, "The Value of Experiencing and Expressing Gratitude," *Ensign*, Mar. 2010.

[12] Henry B. Eyring, "O Remember, Remember," *Ensign*, Nov. 2007.

[13] Henri L. M. Nouwen, *The Return of the Prodigal Son: A Story of Homecoming* (Doubleday, 1994), 86.

[14] Neal A. Maxwell, "Becoming a Disciple," *Ensign*, June 1996.

[15] David A. Bednar, "If Ye Had Known Me," *Ensign*, Nov. 2016.

Chapter 5
Loving-kindness

The Lord is good to all: and His tender mercies are over all His works.

— Psalm 145:9

One of my favorite attributes of God that I have been pondering lately is His loving-kindness. It is a characteristic that best describes who He is and how He feels about His children.

I love the revelation that the Prophet Joseph Smith received that makes up what is known as the "appendix" to the Doctrine and Covenants. In it, this defining attribute of our Heavenly Father is emphasized: "And now the year of my redeemed is come; and they shall mention the loving-kindness of their Lord, and all that he has bestowed upon them according to his goodness, and according to his loving-kindness, forever and ever" (D&C 133:52).

A few years ago, Jens Nielsen from our stake High Council spoke in our ward sacrament meeting. He told about growing up in Denmark, and how his mother died of a brain aneurism when she was 42 and he was just five years old. He described how he was introduced to the Church as a teenager when he lived with a Latter-day Saint family in Idaho, but he wasn't prepared to take the missionary discussions at that time.

Back in Denmark, Jens felt compelled to investigate the Church; and so, between the ages of 17-20, he took the missionary discussions, but he didn't feel prompted to join the Church then.

At the age of 20, he immigrated to America, and began taking the missionary lessons from ward missionaries, Clairon Spencer and Walt Collett, of the Monument Park 16th Ward. After he had been investigating for some time, and the missionaries had almost given up on him, his deceased mother came to him in a dream and encouraged him to accept the gospel message and be baptized.

Jens recognized this as an answer to his prayer, and he promptly joined the Church. He met and married a faithful member of the Church in the Salt Lake Temple, had three children, and settled in Bountiful, Utah. He was the only member of his immediate family to immigrate to America and join the Church.

In 2014, Jens's daughter, Montana, was married in the Salt Lake Temple, and his four brothers from Denmark came to the wedding to support Jens, even though they were not able to enter the temple to witness the marriage of their niece.

While in the sealing room, Jens was suddenly enveloped in a warm hug from behind him—as if being covered by a warm blanket. He felt the presence of his mother, completely encircling him in the arms of her love. He could further sense her approval of the sealing of her granddaughter in the temple of the Lord.

After the ceremony, his eldest brother from Denmark, who is not a member of the Church, could tell that something special had taken place inside the temple. When he asked Jens what had happened, Jens replied in Danish: "I felt the presence of our mother." They both began to cry. A third brother joined their conversation, and he too became emotional when he heard of the spiritual experience Jens had had with their mother, who had passed away decades before.

Jens explained: "We distinctly felt the Holy Spirit burning in our hearts. Here we were, three grown men at Temple Square—all in tears because we could feel our mother's love." For Jens, this truly was a tender mercy of the Lord and an indication of His loving-kindness.

Encircled about eternally in the arms of His love

This experience with the Nielsen family reminds me of Father Lehi's expression: "I am encircled about eternally in the arms of his love" (2 Nephi 1:15).

To fully grasp the meaning of this scripture, visualize the image of a devoted shepherd (our Savior) with a gentle lamb (you, or someone you love) wrapped lovingly in His arms.

Isaiah paints an exquisite picture of this scene: "He shall feed His flock like a shepherd: He shall gather the lambs with His arm, and carry them in His bosom, and shall gently lead those that are with young" (Isaiah 40:11).

In latter-day revelation, this image is again brought to life: "Be faithful and diligent in keeping the commandments of God, and I will encircle thee in the arms of my love" (D&C 6:20).

While reading the biography of Truman Madsen, it's been enlightening to learn that Truman's reliance upon the Lord began when he was a young missionary in the late 1940s serving in the New England States Mission under the direction of President S. Dilworth Young.

President Young asked some of the missionaries to "go without purse or script" for their "country work," just as the disciples did anciently in New Testament times. His objective was for his missionaries to "learn to depend upon the Lord completely."[1]

Truman and his companion were two of the missionaries asked to participate in these summer travels. They were assigned to labor on Prince Edward Island—of *Anne of Green Gables* fame—located off the eastern coast of Canada. They were instructed to "take no thought" as to where to sleep or what to eat, but rather, to rely wholly upon the tender mercies of the Lord and the good graces of the people they were called to teach.

At the end of this experience, Truman was completely "transformed," and he wrote a summary of lessons learned while on "The Island":

- In 2 months [7 July -11 September 1947], the Lord never let us go hungry—we averaged 2 good meals a day [including green apples, raspberries, blueberries—and the fish they caught].
- We learned to pray—"telegram" prayers—sincere and humble.
- We learned to be thankful; thankful for a plate of potatoes, for a bed—we shook people's hands with grateful tears in our eyes.
- We received inspiration—we felt the Lord's directing power.

- We lived the gospel—lived it, ate it, drank it.
- We went through the most strenuous weeks of our lives with a dreamy smile—with heads high.
- It was WONDERFUL—hard, rough, painful, yes—but WONDERFUL.[2]

Although Truman and his companion did not convert a single soul, this hard-earned experience taught them humility and a deep awareness of God's loving- kindness, which, for Truman, served as a well of faith and spiritual confidence throughout his life. "I've gone to the Source for my information," he later wrote his father. "I'm mighty thankful!"[3]

God meets our needs through others

I am a true believer in the principle that President Spencer W. Kimball shared concerning our Heavenly Father's tender care: "God does notice us, and he watches over us. But it is usually through another person that he meets our needs."[4]

While on their missions, both of our sons, Covey and Colin, were the recipients of God's loving-kindness manifested through another person. As a mother who was not present to comfort and bless her missionary sons in their trials, I felt tremendous gratitude when I learned about these tender mercies of the Lord.

Our oldest son, Covey, was called to serve in the Canada Toronto Mission. When he first arrived in Canada, he was assigned to Oakville—a suburb of Toronto. While there, he had the opportunity to teach a man named Darryl Horzelenburg.

Darryl was married to Jodi, the daughter of the stake

president, and he was very familiar with the missionaries, having been approached by them many times. For some reason, this instance was different for Darryl. Covey was able to reach him in a way that other missionaries hadn't been able to, and Darryl was taught and baptized into the Church.

Fast-forward a year later. Covey was now serving in Peterborough and was really struggling. He had a companion who was extremely difficult to get along with, and they were having little success. It all culminated in one miserable night while tracting during a snowfall on Canadian Thanksgiving.

Many of the people who answered their doors were bothered that these two Americans would stop by on a holiday evening. No one wanted to talk to them. The people urged: "Go home and be with your families!" Little did they know how much the missionaries wished they could heed that advice.

As the Elders continued to trudge through the snow, they peered nostalgically into plate glass windows revealing scenes of warm, crackling fires and happy families gathered 'round dinner tables. Oh, how they longed to be shown an ounce of kindness or familiarity!

And then it came . . . a single, solitary voice message from Darryl and Jodi Horzelenburg. "Elder Cole, on this Thanksgiving Day, we just wanted to reach out to let you know that we are thinking of you. We feel so happy and grateful that you brought the gospel into our home, and we will never forget your teachings. Please know how much we love you and miss you."

At this critical juncture of his mission, Covey felt enveloped by the love of the Lord, and it heartened and sustained him. He was warmed with the love from another and was reminded that God was indeed mindful of him.

Our son, Colin, had a similar experience while serving in the Taiwan Taichung Mission. He had spent his first two transfers working in a suburb of Taichung called Zhong Ming. Sometime during that period, his trainer warned him that there was one area that he hoped he would never have to serve in—a township called Xihu.

Colin's companion went on to describe how difficult the area was by saying that it was filled with old people, it required a forty-five-minute bicycle ride to outlying areas, the branch members were not helpful at all, and there had not been a baptism in over two years.

He tried to ease Colin's mind, however, by assuring him that there were over 100 places in which to serve in the mission, and chances were that he would never be sent to this particular location.

Transfers came, and sure enough, Colin was assigned to Xihu. At this point in his mission, he felt anxious, discouraged, and overwhelmed. For one reason, he felt similar to Joseph F. Smith in that he was so young and inexperienced, "he hardly dared look a man in the face."

Colin questioned whether he should have prayed about the timing of when to serve a mission. After all, he was barely eighteen years old when he entered the MTC to learn Mandarin Chinese, and now he was being sent to "the armpit" of the mission. Was he prepared for the trials that awaited him?

Boarding the train, Colin found that every seat was occupied, and so he squeezed his two large suitcases, his backpack, and his carry-on bag into the holding space between the cars and positioned himself against the wall for the four-hour ride to Xihu.

It was an extremely hot and humid day, and Colin was wearing his jacket to free up luggage space. As he uncomfortably stood there, perspiration trickling down his face, he pulled out the *Book of Mormon*, and began perusing the pages. As he did so, doubts and worries arose in his mind. He inwardly questioned: "Is all this worth it for the book?"

Suddenly, a man standing near to Colin did something that was very uncharacteristic of a Taiwanese person. He took the book out of his hands and began thumbing through its pages. The man then looked directly at Colin and remarked in Mandarin: "This is a very good book. What you are doing is a good work."

Colin recorded in his journal: "Those were the words he said, but what I heard was the voice of my Heavenly Father, saying: *I know who you are. I am aware of your struggles. There is a reason you are going to this area. I love you, and I will help you.*"

This encounter was a turning point for Colin. At the exact moment he needed confirmation that he was where he was supposed to be, performing the work with which he had been entrusted, God reached out to him in loving-kindness to reassure him of his purpose.

Colin ended up having a marvelous experience in this "dreaded" area. He and his companion were able to find and baptize a young adult who soon became an Elder and has since received his endowment. They also found many potential converts and brought them to church, and duly activated a less-active young man who has since gone on a mission.

At some point in our lives, we will all find ourselves on

the train to Xihu, so to speak— burdened, heavy laden—not with luggage and personal belongings, but with grief or worry or doubt. Yet, if we are humble and prayerful, we too, will receive an assurance from God that we are not alone, and He is by our side.

Elder David A. Bednar reminds: "We should not underestimate or overlook the power of the Lord's tender mercies. The simplicity, the sweetness, and the constancy of the tender mercies of the Lord will do much to fortify and protect us in the troubled times in which we do now and will yet live."[5]

The Lord will remember His covenant

If there is one thing I have learned from my study of the scriptures, it is that God fulfills His promises to His children. If we keep His commandments, we will prosper. If we don't keep His commandments, we will perish. We can point to instance after instance in the *Book of Mormon* which illustrates this principle.

When my father was serving as a mission president in Ireland, he had an experience that profoundly affected him. Over a period of months, he had been studying the Atonement of Jesus Christ in great depth in an effort to comprehend the infinite love God has for each of His children.

One night, after touring the mission for several days, Dad hurried back to the mission home in Belfast, Northern Ireland, hoping to greet us children before we went to bed. Unfortunately, when he arrived home, he found it was too late: the house was dark, and we were sound asleep.

Our father crept into each of our bedrooms and knelt

by our bedsides. Similar to the *Book of Mormon* prophet, Enos, he prayed through the night and was literally filled with the love of God.

Initially, he felt to pray for his family and those living within the mission home; then, his prayer extended towards the members of the Church in Ireland; and finally, he felt charity—the pure love of Christ—for every Irish soul. For just a moment, he comprehended in the most infinitesimal way, the love that enabled our Heavenly Father to offer His Beloved Son as a sacrifice for sin.

And then our father blessed us. He blessed Cynthia, age five, and me, age two, with the promise that we would one day return to Ireland as missionaries.

Fast-forward sixteen years. Cynthia submitted her mission papers to Church headquarters and received her call to serve in the Ireland Dublin Mission—Church leaders being completely unaware of the blessing our father had given her.

Three years after that, when I turned 21, I, too, was called to serve in the Ireland Dublin Mission—again, with no foreknowledge or intervention.

Our father did not even mention the blessings he had pronounced upon our heads until many years after we had returned from our missions to Ireland. Due to these experiences and others, I have no doubt that God is aware of each of His children and fulfills His promises to them.

Understanding this principle gives us power and purpose. Truman Madsen wrote: "No religion in the whole world, stresses so much the meaning and worth of the individual. Individuality is the ultimate value; the Church is the instrument for its fulfillment; the family is the highest expression of individual life, even the Divine

Life." [6] What a beautiful and true expression about the divine worth of each soul!

I have a dear friend, Meg Benson Ferry, who served in the Italy Rome Mission. After she married and began her family, she spoke a great deal of Italian to her young children, with the hope that they would develop an ear for the language.

Meg and her grandfather, President Ezra Taft Benson, share the same birthday: August 4th. At President Benson's 88th and Meg's 28th birthday party, Meg's oldest daughter, Laura—then two years old—sang "Happy Birthday" to her great-grandpa in Italian.

He was so delighted that he made a promise to her: "When you grow up, Laura, you will fulfill a mission to Rome, Italy, just like your mother did." Meg noted his words, recorded them, and like Mary, the mother of Jesus, "kept all these things, and pondered them in her heart" (see Luke 2:19).

Throughout junior high and high school, Laura developed a desire to serve a fulltime mission. Just as she was completing her degrees in violin performance and Italian at the University of Maryland, Laura submitted her mission papers from her Young Single Adult (YSA) ward—20 years after the noted birthday party of her mother and great-grandfather, who had died 12 years earlier. Meg had never told Laura what President Benson had said to her at their shared birthday party because she wanted Laura to exercise her agency and to choose her own path.

When the envelope containing Laura's mission call arrived in the dorm mail, she called home to open her call over the phone with her family. No surprise to her mother, Laura was called to serve in the Italy Rome Mission!

It was during that conversation that Meg shared with Laura what President Benson had prophesied 20 years earlier.

In response, Laura revealed a related dream she had had the previous night.

While asleep in her dorm room, Laura experienced what she described as a prophetic vision—much like Lehi's vision of the Tree of Life. In the dream, she was sitting with her great-grandfather. Together, they were looking through a large book, flipping through its pages as if it were an enormous photo album—perhaps even the Book of Life.

President Benson lovingly said to Laura, "Dear Granddaughter, you will walk the streets of Italy that your mother walked and serve the people of Italy that she served. I have gone before a council of angels in heaven and petitioned that you be sent to Italy on your mission." When Laura awoke from that very clear and powerful dream, she was weeping. That very day, she received her call to the Italy Rome Mission. She ultimately served in many of the same cities where her mother, Meg, had served.

Now living in the Kirtland Stake with her husband and two young children, Laura continues to treasure her grandfather's prophetic statement and the revelatory dream she had. She feels great peace in the knowledge that our Heavenly Father knows and loves her and has a plan for her life.

Indeed, "the Lord will remember His covenant which he hath made unto His people of the house of Israel" (3 Ne. 29:3).

You are deeply loved and cared for

The concept of God as our loving Heavenly Father is nowhere better manifest than in the novel, *City of Tranquil Light*, by Bo Caldwell. Honestly, reading this book was like coming home to me. There is no more stunning writing or spiritual expression than in this story about a Mennonite young man who gives himself over to God and who allows himself to be molded and shaped by Him.

Maybe because this story is about a Christian missionary who serves nearly his entire life in China, or perhaps because I, too, have a son who feels that his life's work is in China, I have been profoundly affected by the premise of this book. Regardless of the reason, the main character, Will Keen, describes so beautifully the loving-kindness of our Heavenly Father that I felt compelled to include this excerpt:

"Again, and again, my ancestors said 'yes' to God, and as I grew I saw those around me say 'yes' as well. Over the months then years I watched one person after another in our community walk forward at Sunday services. At times I looked wistfully, even enviously, at the new church members and wished that I, too, could say the words, could produce the faith. But I could not; I was suspicious of God and was afraid that, if I said 'yes' to Him, He would change me in ways I would not like and ask of me things I did not want to do. I thought of the visiting missionary, and of what I had felt as he spoke. What if God should ask me to leave home? That I could never do. So, I tolerated the restlessness that dwelt in my heart and decided that faith could wait.

"Which it did, for four years, until early one morning in late summer when I was in the fields. I was sixteen years old and farming was what I loved. . .

"That morning I fell to my knees behind the plow to pray before I began the day's work, just as I did every morning, for while I was unable to surrender myself to God, I was equally unable to turn my back on Him, and I could not discard my habit of cautious prayer. The day was already hot, and the sun warmed my back as I knelt in the cool red dirt and thanked God for my life and asked Him to help me plow a straight line.

"I was about to stand when something stopped me. It was the quiet, a deep calm that I did not want to leave or disturb. I stayed very still, and as I gazed out at the wide expanse of rich red earth, my mind and heart grew still as well. I felt a Presence that seemed to surround me and pursue me at the same time, a Presence that I knew was God, and I had the sense that I was deeply loved and cared for. I had been told of this love since I was small, but on that morning it seemed to move from my head into my heart; knowledge became belief.

"As I remained kneeling in the red soil, it seemed that the gift of faith was being offered to me. I whispered, 'Help me to believe,' and a feeling of great relief came over me as I realized how I had been longing for enough faith to give myself over. From somewhere inside I felt a 'yes,' and an unfamiliar peace replaced the restlessness in my soul."[7]

Many years after Will internalizes the profound love God has for him, he is prompted by the Spirit to accompany a visiting missionary back to China. At this stage of his life, Will has little confidence in his ability to make any sort of difference in the life of another, yet he does have faith in God and in his ability to make something out of him.

The rest of the story describes the selfless service and the subsequent transformation of a young man into a powerful and effective missionary—all beginning with the knowledge that he is known of and loved by the Lord.

In his autobiography, *Proof of Heaven*, Dr. Eben Alexander, the neurosurgeon whose Spirit left his body while suffering a rare illness—only to be restored to life again—discovered when he was taken up to heaven that the one thing that truly matters is love.

Dr. Alexander explains:

"I had initially received this piece of knowledge from my lovely companion on the butterfly wing upon my first entrance into the Gateway. It came in three parts, and to take one more shot at putting it into words (because of course it was initially delivered wordlessly), it would run something like this:

You are loved and cherished.

You have nothing to fear.

There is nothing you can do wrong.

If I had to boil this entire message down to one sentence, it would run this way:

You are loved.

And if I had to boil it down further, to just one word, it would (of course) be, simply:

Love."

During his near-death experience and his visit to the Spirit World, Dr. Alexander was taught in a very personal way, "love is, without a doubt, the basis of everything."[8]

Isn't it telling that the Apostle Paul and Moroni also chose this attribute of love, or charity, as the greatest characteristic of all? It is "the pure love of Christ, and it endureth forever; and whoso is found possessed of it at the last day, it shall be well with him" (Moroni 7:47).

When God extends His love to us, we become filled with this charity, and we are able to love Him—and others—in return. This miracle is brought to pass because of the principle that John the Beloved taught: "We love Him because He first loved us" (1 John 4:19). As our Heavenly Father offers His loving-kindness to each of us, we partake of His divine nature and become more like Him.

I conclude this chapter with the summarizing words of Will Keen, the fictional character in *City of Tranquil Light*, who, when looking back on his life, recognizes the hand of God in every step of his path, and acknowledges His ubiquitous loving-kindness:

"Over time I have come to believe that God's will is a mystery, fluid and surprising. Following it is like stepping out into something I cannot see, and I am frequently unsure about whether I am doing God's will until after the fact.

"But I have learned that while I don't always know when I'm doing something right, I always know when I'm doing something wrong, and I rely on this as I go forward, trusting that He will use my mistakes as well as my triumphs and knowing that He does not ask me to be perfect, or even good. He simply asks me to be His, which to me is the heart of His Good News: that I am deeply and passionately loved exactly as I am, despite the faults that grieve me most, by a God who delights in me more than I can know—a God who created me so He could love me.

"With the gift of that renewed certainty when I awake

each morning, I rise to meet the day and to praise my dear Lord, and to finish my course with joy."[9]

Initiatives to consider

1) God's loving-kindness is one of His most defining characteristics. Ponder on the Apostle John's teaching that "we love Him because He first loved us."

2) Father Lehi describes being "encircled about eternally in the arms of His love" (2 Nephi 1: 15). Identify times in your life when you have personally experienced these tender mercies of the Lord.

3) God knows and loves each of His children perfectly and personally. How does it make you feel to know that you are deeply and passionately loved exactly as you are?

---

[1] Barnard N. Madsen, *The Truman G. Madsen Story: A Life of Study and Faith* (Deseret Book, 2016), 141.

[2] *Ibid*, 137-138.

[3] *Ibid*, 141.

[4] Spencer W. Kimball, "Small Acts of Service," *Ensign*, Dec. 1974.

[5] David A. Bednar, "The Tender Mercies of the Lord," *Ensign*, May 2005.

[6] Lucinda A. Barnhurst manuscript for *BYU Today*, 1 Nov. 1981; Journal 1981.

[7] Bo Caldwell, *City of Tranquil Light* (St. Martin's Griffin, 2010), 8.

[8] Eben Alexander, *Proof of Heaven* (Simon & Schuster, 2012), 70-71.

[9] Bo Caldwell, *City of Tranquil Light* (St. Martin's Griffin, 2010), 282-283.

Chapter 6
Salvation

A man filled with the love of God is not content with blessing his family alone, but ranges through the whole world anxious to bless the whole human race.

— Joseph Smith

Our family goes through a ritual when dropping off missionaries at the MTC. After saying our brief goodbyes, and just as the missionary is being whisked off by their greeter at the curb, we pump our fists in the air and shout three times in unison, "Hurrah, hurrah for Israel."

The inception of this tradition came from a family trip to Nauvoo when our children were quite young. While there, we learned that the members of the Quorum of the Twelve Apostles were commanded to go to England in 1839 to preach the gospel. When the time came to depart, many Apostles and their families were suffering from malaria and shaking with fever. Regardless, the Apostles were determined to obey the Lord's command, trusting that He would care for them.

One particular account brought us to tears. We've

reflected on it again and again, knowing that we would never look on missionary work in the same way. It is the story of Brigham Young and Heber C. Kimball when they left their families and homes to journey to Great Britain to fulfill their mission calls.

Heber C. Kimball recorded the event in these words:

"September 18th, 1839: Charles Hubbard sent his boy with a wagon and span of horses to my house; our trunks were put into the wagon by some brethren; I went to my bed and shook hands with my wife who was then shaking with a chill, having two children lying sick by her side; I embraced her and my children, and bade them farewell. My only well child was little Heber P., and it was with difficulty he could carry a couple of quarts of water at a time to assist in quenching their thirst.

"It was with difficulty we got into the wagon and started down the hill about ten rods; it appeared to me as though my very inmost parts would melt within me at leaving my family in such a condition, as it were almost in the arms of death. I felt as though I could not endure it. I asked the teamster to stop, and said to Brother Brigham, "This is pretty tough, isn't it; let's rise up and give them a cheer."

"We arose, and swinging our hats three times over our heads, shouted: "Hurrah, hurrah for Israel." Vilate, hearing the noise, arose from her bed and came to the door. She had a smile on her face. Vilate and Mary Ann Young cried out to us: "Goodbye, God bless you!"

"We returned the compliment, and then told the driver to go ahead. After this I felt a spirit of joy and gratitude, having had the satisfaction of seeing my wife standing upon her feet, instead of leaving her in bed, knowing well

that I should not see them again for two or three years."[1]

The resolve shown by Brigham and Heber in this instance is characteristic of the commitment of these early brethren and their families who sacrificed *all* for the Kingdom of God. Their primary motivation was to give hope and reason to hardship and separation, and their jubilant cheer did just that.

Hence, in these latter days, when we join in shouting, "Hurrah, hurrah for Israel," in the face of our departing missionaries, it's as though we embrace that very sacrifice with joy and gratitude, trusting that He will care for us too.

Missionary work and how it saves us

Jennifer Tolk, a sister in my ward, shared a story about a boy in her Primary class who bore his testimony in sacrament meeting. When she complimented him on it afterwards, the boy replied in all earnestness: "I felt that as I spoke, my sins were forgiven me."

This is actually true doctrine. Bearing our testimonies/sharing the gospel will literally "save us" and "hide a multitude of sins." I have made a study of scriptures that support this principle, and I am astounded by the blessings promised to those who are willing to open their mouths. Below is just a sampling of such promises:

- Mosiah 28:7: "And the Lord said unto Mosiah: Let them go up, for many shall believe on their words, *and they shall have eternal life*; and I will deliver thy sons out of the hands of the Lamanites."
- D&C 4:4: "For behold the field is white already to harvest; and lo, he that thrusteth in his sickle with his might, the same layeth up in store that he

perisheth not, *but bringeth salvation to his soul.*"

- D&C 12:3: "Behold, the field is white already to harvest; therefore, whoso desireth to reap let him thrust in his sickle with his might, and reap while the day lasts, *that he may treasure up for his soul everlasting salvation in the kingdom of God.*"
- D&C 31:5: "Therefore, thrust in your sickle with all your soul, *and your sins are forgiven you,* and you shall be laden with sheaves upon your back, for the laborer is worthy of his hire. Wherefore, your family shall live."
- D&C 62:3: "Nevertheless, ye are blessed, for the testimony which ye have borne is recorded in heaven for the angels to look upon; and they rejoice over you, *and your sins are forgiven you.*"
- D&C 84:61: "*For I will forgive you of your sins with this commandment*—that you remain steadfast in your minds in solemnity and the spirit of prayer, in bearing testimony to all the world of those things which are communicated unto you."
- James 5:20: "Let him know, that he which converteth the sinner from the error of his way shall save a soul from death and *shall hide a multitude of sins.*"
- Ezekiel 33:16: "*None of his sins that he hath committed shall be mentioned unto him*: he hath done that which is lawful and right; he shall surely live."

I find this doctrine to be extremely redeeming and comforting, not only for the fulltime missionary but also for the rank and file member of the Church. In other words, what these scriptures are saying is that "notwithstanding our weakness" (see 2 Nephi 33:11), our sins are forgiven us— *if* we will bear our testimony and share the gospel with those around us.

Missionary work and the concept of redeeming other lost or fallen souls

President Dallin H. Oaks taught that regardless of the circumstances we find ourselves in, there are three things Latter-day Saints can do to help share the gospel:

First, we can pray for the desire to help with this vital part of the work of salvation. All efforts begin with desire.

Second, we can keep the commandments ourselves. Faithful, obedient members are the most persuasive witnesses of the truth and value of the restored gospel.

Third, we can pray for inspiration on what we can do in our individual circumstances to share the gospel with others. We should pray for what we can do personally.

When we pray, we should remember that prayers for inspiration will be answered if accompanied by "real intent" or "full purpose of heart."

Finally, we must pray with a commitment to act upon the inspiration [we] receive, promising the Lord that if He will inspire [us] to speak to someone about the gospel, [we] will do it.[2]

In addition, and perhaps most importantly, we must remember that redemption is found in Jesus Christ, for it is only through His name and His infinite atoning sacrifice that we can be saved. Hence, the fullness of our intent to share the gospel is to invite all the children of men to come unto Christ and "partake of His salvation, and the power of His redemption" (Omni 1:26). Like Nephi, "we labor diligently to write, to persuade our children, and also our brethren, to believe in Christ, and to be reconciled to God" (2 Nephi 25:23).

Lose your life to find it

When Elder Gordon B. Hinckley first arrived in the mission field as a young man, he was assigned to labor in Preston, England. Within a short time, he became disheartened by a lack of interest in and opposition to the Church and the gospel message.

As a result of this discouragement, Elder Hinckley wrote a letter to his father explaining that he was wasting his time and his father's money. Not long afterwards, Elder Hinckley received a response from his dad. It read, "Dear Gordon, I have your recent letter. I have only one suggestion: forget yourself and go to work."

During his personal study that very morning, Elder Hinckley had read the following teaching of the Savior: "Whosoever will save his life shall lose it; but whosoever shall lose his life for my sake and the gospel's, the same shall save it" (Mark 8:35).

"Those words of the Master, followed by my father's letter with his counsel to forget myself and go to work, went into my very being.

With my father's letter in hand, I went into our bedroom in the house at 15 Wadham Road, where we lived, and got on my knees and made a pledge with the Lord. I covenanted that I would try to forget myself and lose myself in His service."[3]

He was true to his word. Since that "day of decision" in 1933, Gordon B. Hinckley honored this solemn promise throughout his life and during his service as the 15th President of The Church of Jesus Christ of Latter-day Saints.

An additional verse in the New Testament underscores this principle: "For whosoever will save his life shall lose it: but whosoever will lose his life for my sake, the same shall save it" (Luke 9:24).

President Thomas S. Monson said of this scripture:

"I believe the Savior is telling us that unless we lose ourselves in service to others, there is little purpose to our own lives. Those who live only for themselves eventually shrivel up and figuratively lose their lives, while those who lose themselves in service to others grow and flourish—and in effect save their lives."[4]

Fulltime missionaries throughout the world who literally lose their lives in the service of their fellow man continue to inspire me. Isn't it interesting that at the time of life when a young person is usually the most self-centered, the Lord asks them to forget themselves and to serve Him and His other children for eighteen months to two years?

In the meanwhile, these missionaries are working harder than they ever have, getting up earlier than they ever have, putting in 12 to 14-hour days, paying for their own expenses, forgoing school, work, and personal relationships—in essence forgetting their lives. And yet, despite their sacrifice, they have never been happier! This illustration teaches us, lay members of the Church, where true happiness and contentment is ultimately found.

Continue to minister

While serving as a missionary in Cork, Ireland, I had a District Leader who was a fairly recent convert to the Church. His name was Elder Jess Askeroth. He was an excellent leader and a diligent missionary, and I was extremely impressed by his work ethic and commitment.

On one occasion, Elder Askeroth shared his conversion story with our district. He told how he was living with his family in Minnesota when they met the missionaries, took the discussions, and were baptized into the Church. Jess was 17 years old at the time, and although he felt prompted to become a member, he lost contact with the Church soon after graduation when he left home and enrolled in the U.S. Air Force.

Many years later, now in his early twenties, Jess moved to Las Vegas on assignment. Since his name was still on the rolls of the Church, local church authorities contacted him and reached out in fellowship to reactive him. The Bishop of the resident ward and his family took a personal interest in Jess, and they invited him into their home.

This family's warmth and commitment helped rekindle the flame of testimony that had once burned within him. Jess became fully active in the Church and decided to serve a mission.

Elder Askeroth went on to say that because these fellow Saints had not given up on him, they literally saved him, and now he had come on a mission to help save others. He had a favorite scripture, characteristic of his situation, which he loved to share:

"Nevertheless, ye shall not cast him out of your synagogues, or your places of worship, for unto such shall ye continue to minister; for ye know not but what they will return and repent, and come unto me with full purpose of heart, and I shall heal them; and ye shall be the means of bringing salvation unto them (3 Nephi 18:32)."

To "be the means of bringing salvation" unto one of our Heavenly Father's children is perhaps the most valuable gift a person can give and is a source of great joy (see D&C 18:15). Although we may not see the fruit of our labors immediately, "continuing to minister" is the key to helping a fellow member "return and repent," and turn unto God "with full purpose of heart."

Elder Kazuhiko Yamashita of the Seventy gave a beautiful talk in general conference about this subject, entitled "Be Ambitious for Christ." He shared a personal story about his less-engaged son who responded to his loved one's efforts to minister to him, and how the Lord healed him in the process:

"Our second son lived much of his youth apart from the Church. When he turned 20, he had an experience that made him want to change his life. With love, prayers, and help from his family and members of the Church, and ultimately through the compassion and grace of the Lord, he returned to the Church.

"He was later called to serve in the Washington Seattle Mission. He initially suffered great discouragement. Every night for the first three months, he would go into the bathroom and cry . . . He sought to understand "Why am I here?"

"After he served for a year, we received an email that was an answer to our prayers. He wrote: "Right now I can really feel the love of God and of Jesus. I will work hard to become like the prophets of old. Though I am also experiencing a lot of difficulties, I am truly happy. Serving Jesus really is the best thing ever. There is nothing as wonderful as this. I am so happy."[5]

Analogous to Alma the Younger, who also returned and repented, this young man's family did not give up on him but continued to minister until he fully experienced the "joy" and the "marvelous light" found in the healing power of the Atonement of Jesus Christ (see Alma 36:20).

Truth will prevail

When the Latter-day Saint missionaries first sailed into Liverpool, England, in 1837, they petitioned God for assistance and direction, and their pleas did not go unheeded. They felt guided by the Spirit to begin their work in nearby Preston.

The Elders arrived in Preston on a "public day," a holiday of sorts, held prior to a parliamentary election under the newly crowned, Queen Victoria. Festivities included a parade and marching bands, with throngs of people celebrating in the public square.

Descending from their coach, they looked up to see a banner unfurled from a window above them, proclaiming in bold gilt letters: "Truth Will Prevail."[6]

Taking it as a sign from heaven of good things to come, the missionaries immediately adopted this as the motto of their mission, and it became a widely used phrase throughout the Church.

One Elder, Jacob Gates, reporting on his mission to Indiana, wrote in a letter published in Nauvoo's *Times and*

Seasons in 1841: "Although the Lord has chosen the weak things of this world to preach his gospel, truth will prevail, and will prosper."[7]

These early missionaries had faith, and produced evidence, that truth would indeed prevail and would prosper. Despite the trials the Latter-day Saints have endured, and have yet to endure, we have no need to fear. An Apostle of the Lord has declared: "This is God's work, and God's work will not be frustrated."[8]

We are all familiar with the prophetic words of Joseph Smith: "The Standard of Truth has been erected; no unhallowed hand can stop the work from progressing; persecutions may rage, mobs may combine, armies may assemble, calumny may defame, but the truth of God will go forth boldly, nobly, and independent, till it has penetrated every continent, visited every clime, swept every country, and sounded in every ear, till the purposes of God shall be accomplished, and the Great Jehovah shall say the work is done."[9]

Nearly two centuries have passed since the restoration of the Lord's Church upon the earth. We have been privileged to witness the fulfillment of prophecy as "the truth of God" has gone "forth boldly, nobly, and independent." There is still much work to be done, and now *we* are the ones entrusted to carry it forward. Let us not shrink from our duty, but rather be faithful and diligent in hastening the work of salvation.

Initiatives to consider

1. How does knowing that when bearing your testimony, "your sins will be forgiven you" serve as motivation for sharing the gospel?
2. Prayerfully consider certain individuals to whom you may "continue to minister."
3. Similar to President Hinckley, have you experienced a "day of decision" when you pledged to lose yourself in the service of the Lord? If not, how can you come to such a day?

---

[1] L. Tom Perry, "United in Building the Kingdom of God," *Ensign,* April 1987.

[2] Dallin H. Oaks, "Sharing the Restored Gospel," *Ensign*, Nov. 2016.

[3] Gordon B. Hinckley, "Taking the Gospel to Britain," *Ensign,* July 1987.

[4] Thomas S. Monson, "What Have I Done for Someone Today?" *Ensign,* Nov. 2009.

[5] Kazuhiko Yamashita, "Be Ambitious for Christ," *Ensign*, Nov. 2016.

[6] Heber C. Kimball Diary, July 1837; Joseph Fielding Diary, July 1837, Church Archives.

[7] Oliver Mayall, "Truth Will Prevail," *New Era*, Sept. 2010.

[8] M. Russell Ballard, "The Truth of God Shall Go Forth," *Ensign*, Nov. 2008.

[9] Joseph Smith, *History of the Church,* 4:540.

Chapter 7
Greatness

Everyone has the power for greatness—not for fame but greatness, because greatness is determined by service.
> — *Dr. Martin Luther King, Jr.*

Of late, I've been reading the excellent biographies of Alexander Hamilton and George Washington by historian Ron Chernow. It's fascinating to learn about those who served as leaders in the pursuit of American independence, both on the field of battle and within the chambers of government. While none of these individuals were perfect, God raised them up to lay the foundation of a nation where the Church of Jesus Christ of Latter-day Saints could be restored.

It is remarkable that in a country with a population of only 2.5 million people (during the late 1700s), an array of the most prepared, the most educated, and the most courageous men and women lived. Surely, these individuals were uniquely prepared by God to do the work they were called upon to perform.

My mother taught my siblings and me to revere the

Founding Fathers of our nation. She revealed to us what it actually meant to the signers of the Declaration of Independence to pledge their lives, their fortunes, and their sacred honor. This was literal. If the British captured any one of these signers—and many were caught—they would be tortured and killed for their rebellious act of treason. To the Founders and their families who sacrificed so inordinately for their country, greatness *was* service.

It's no wonder that some of the first spirits who requested that their ordinance work be done, once a temple of the Lord was built, were the great men and women of our country's founding who appeared to Temple President Wilford Woodruff within the sacred walls of the St. George Temple.

As per their request, the vicarious ordinances for the signers of the Declaration of Independence as well as for many other Founding Fathers, Presidents of the United States, and "eminent women" (of whom there were seventy!), were performed in 1877.[1]

After he became the Prophet, President Woodruff declared: "Those men [and women] who laid the foundation of this American government were the best spirits the God of heaven could find on the face of the earth. They were choice spirits [and] were inspired of the Lord."[2]

More substance to our souls

What has become apparent to me about these noble men and women is that they were caught up in a cause bigger than themselves. They became significant not because they pursued fame or success, but rather, because they *served* their way to greatness. President Spencer W. Kimball explained:

"The more we serve our fellowmen in appropriate ways, the more substance there is to our souls. We become more significant individuals as we serve others. We become more substantive as we serve others—indeed, it is easier to 'find' ourselves because there is so much more of us to find!"[3]

There is a scene in Saint-Exupery's *The Little Prince* where the fox says: 'What's essential is invisible.' And so it is with this large subject of character: to a very great extent, it is invisible. It has to do with aspects of individual integrity for which there are no ready measurements—the honor of General Washington, Lincoln's depth of soul, the resolution of John Adams.

Or consider the faith of the early Saints in the face of adversity, or the courage of the Prophet Joseph Smith when surrounded by a mob or in almost any situation.

The invisible something each of these individuals brought to their circumstance was character. Historian David McCullough reminds: "History teaches that character counts. Character above all."[4]

Primary vs. secondary greatness

One of the most influential teachings of my childhood was the focus on primary vs. secondary greatness. My father taught us that the world is consumed with what he termed "secondary greatness," i.e., social recognition for talents, good looks, possessions, positions, and so on; whereas "primary greatness" indicates a goodness of heart and character—when a person's fundamental nature is based upon their integrity, service, and faith. Dad would often say: "What we *are* communicates far more eloquently than anything we *say or do.*"[5]

In writing to teens about this concept, my brother Sean tells of an experience he had when playing the starting quarterback position at BYU. He writes about one particular game early in the season when he was really struggling with energy and focus. By halftime, he had already thrown two interceptions.

During halftime, one of the coaches warned him that he better produce on the next drive or be replaced by back-up quarterback, Ty Detmer. (Nothing like having the future Heisman Trophy winner as your understudy!)

The offense sputtered on the next two possessions, and sure enough Sean was taken out of the game. He silently fumed, as he had never been benched—not even for one drive—during his entire playing career. Ty was able to rally the team, and BYU defeated UTEP. Of course, Sean was happy for the win, but embarrassed by being pulled. And to top it off—it was his birthday—the worst one ever!

After the game, members of the media began filing into the locker room. The reporters called out a brief "hello" to Sean as they rushed back to interview Ty. Just two weeks later, Sean would be the 'hero,' throwing for 360 yards and two touchdowns in a victory over Utah State. Today, he was the 'goat,' and no one wanted to talk to him.

It ended up being a roller coaster of a season for Sean—with emotions high one moment, low the next. Sports reporters and fans praised him one game, cursed him the next.

Just one week after a huge win against TCU where he passed for 490 yards, Sean found himself in the hospital undergoing orthoscopic surgery for tearing some cartilage in his knee. From this point on, his knee was never the same, and he ended up needing an ACL repair by the end of the year.

In the midst of this tumultuous football season, Sean experienced a life-changing epiphany. He realized that if he were to base his self-esteem and his feelings of self-worth on any source other than the quality of his heart and his identity as a son of God, he was basing it on a very shaky footing.

Sean came to recognize the importance of "building our foundation on Christ and his gospel, because everything else—relationships, health, circumstances, [sports]—can be fickle, volatile, unpredictable, and unstable."[6]

On the other hand, building our foundation upon the Savior makes us, in the words of Elder Neal A. Maxwell, "grounded, rooted, established, and settled."[7] Ultimately, "primary" or "true" greatness is about character—the quality of a person's heart, mind, or soul, which cannot be altered.

Show courage and character in defining moments

One of the most poignant examples I know of a person who possessed "primary greatness" is the story told by Kitty De Ruyter-Bons about her mother, Anna, in her autobiography, *As I Have Loved You*.

Kitty and her family were raised in very comfortable circumstances in Dutch Indonesia until the Japanese invaded their island paradise of Java during World War II. Soon after the invasion, all of the Euro-Asian men of the community were rounded up and forced into concentration camps.

Kitty's father was one of those taken prisoner, although he escaped and formed a resistance movement. He was later recaptured and spent the entire Japanese occupation apart from his family, leaving Anna and her six children to fend for themselves. Kitty was amazed by her mother's resolution and resourcefulness during this period, despite extreme hardship and deprivation.

Not long after the men were imprisoned, the Euro-Asian women and children of this island nation were also sent to prison camps. Kitty's older brothers were separated from the family and sent off with the men, while she and her three younger sisters and baby brother were sent to a camp with their mother and the other women.

While imprisoned, Anna, who was a devout Christian, was warned that she was not allowed to pray to God; nevertheless, she began each day with prayer and taught her children all that she remembered of the scriptures. She invited their fellow prison mates to join with them in daily worship.

Because of her natural leadership ability, Anna was chosen to be the barracks unit leader. On one occasion, she was ordered to prepare twenty-eight young women between the ages of fourteen and twenty-two to be used as prostitutes for the Japanese officers, who were celebrating a holiday. Knowing this was an abomination in the sight of God, she fasted and prayed, and felt impressed to shave off the hair from these women's heads and rub a stinky root from a noxious weed all over their bodies, so they would be doubly unappealing to the Japanese officers.

When the officers discovered Anna's defiant act, they were furious and beat her savagely; they ripped off her clothes as well as the clothes of the other women who had helped her and insulted and shamed her. When asked why she had defied their orders, Anna courageously replied: "My God has sanctified some things in our lives. Virtue is one of these . . . We will protect this virtue at all costs, even unto death. As one of the leaders here, I will take responsibility for the action I have taken."[8]

As a consequence, Anna was sentenced to two weeks in "the pit"—an open ditch, covered by chicken wire and exposed to the elements, not wide enough to lie down in— a brutal punishment that often proved fatal for the prisoner.

When Anna was dragged away, she reminded her children how Jesus had asked his disciples to "watch and pray" for him when he went into the Garden of Gethsemane. In effect, Anna was signaling that being confined to "the pit" was her equivalent of "Gethsemane," and she needed an abundance of their faith and prayers. Her children did not disappoint, but rather, were faithful and prayerful.

Remarkably, Anna survived, but was severely weakened by this ordeal. On the evening she was freed from "the pit," she painfully waited in line to receive her rations of food and water. Anna's nine-year-old daughter, Kitty, later recorded the following interchange with a Japanese soldier:

"Seeing my mother like that fueled the hatred in my heart for those responsible, and I forgot my mother's teachings and lost control. When I passed one of the officers who handed out our rations, I threw my cup of precious drinking water in his face and spat at him. Then I said the most unkind words I could think of.

"Immediately, a samurai sword was drawn towards me. Quickly, my mother put her hands on the sword and pushed it away from me, cutting her hands in the process.

"'Please pick up your cup, Kitty, and apologize,' she begged me softly. But I stood there frozen with fear. I knew that when a soldier draws a samurai sword, he will use it—and I feared the worst.

"In those moments, my mother taught me the true virtue of charity. She became my mediator, as Jesus Christ is for each of us. With great difficulty she bent and picked up the cup, then bowed deeply, as was required when addressing the Japanese. She offered apologies in my name, ex-plaining that I was only a child and had not acquired the discipline to master my emotions, and she asked the Japanese officer to please have mercy on me. 'If there must be a punishment,' she said, 'I will take it for my child.'

"After a long searching look at my mother, the officer slowly put the sword back in its sheath, gently took the cup from my mother's hands and filled it with water. 'Woman, drink!' he said, and surprised but grateful, my mother drank the water. . .

"With a slight bow, which is a sign of respect, the officer said, 'It is I who must apologize to you for not recognizing the majesty of your womanhood.' Her courageous interference had awakened in him the realization that this war had made a savage out of him . . . as he was about to lower himself to strike and hurt a child.

"My mother bent her head toward him. 'Truly, you

have the spirit of Ishido ["warrior with great wisdom"] in you!' she reciprocated. In this my mother showed us that she was wise, and also that she was educated . . . Truly she taught us to 'Love your enemies and do good . . . hoping for nothing again; and your reward shall be great, and ye shall be the children of the Highest: for he is kind unto the unthankful and to the evil' [Luke 6:35]."[9]

Anna was blessed for her goodness and character, and she and her children were safeguarded. Even the Japanese soldier who exercised authority over her sensed her nobility of spirit and felt to acknowledge it.

A similar occurrence, which also illustrates great courage and character, is the story of the Prophet Joseph Smith and other brethren who were unjustly imprisoned in Richmond Jail. Fellow prisoner, Parley P. Pratt, described the setting in this way:

"In one of those tedious nights we had lain as if in sleep, till the hour of midnight has passed, and our ears and hearts had been pained, while we had listened for hours to the obscene jests, the horrid oaths, the dreadful blasphemies, and filthy language of our guards, Col. Price at their head, as they recounted to each other their deeds of rapine, murder, robbery, etc., which they had committed among the 'Mormons,' while at Far West, and vicinity. They even boasted of defiling by force, wives, daughters, and virgins, and of shooting or dashing out the brains of men, women, and children.

"I had listened till I became so disgusted, shocked, horrified, and so filled with the spirit of indignant justice, that I could scarcely refrain from rising upon my feet and rebuking the guards, but had said nothing to Joseph, or anyone else, although I lay next to him and knew he was awake. On a sudden he arose to his feet, and spoke in a voice of thunder, or as the roaring lion, uttering, as near as I can recollect, the following words:

"'SILENCE—Ye fiends of the infernal pit. In the name of Jesus Christ, I rebuke you, and command you to be still; I will not live another minute and hear such language. Cease such talk, or you or I die THIS MINUTE.'

"He ceased to speak. He stood erect in terrible majesty. Chained, and without a weapon—calm, unruffled and dignified as an angel, he looked down upon the quailing guards, whose weapons were lowed or dropped to the ground; whose knees smote together, and who, shrinking into a corner, or crouching at his feet, begged his pardon, and remained quiet till a change of guards.

"I have seen the ministers of justice, clothed in magisterial robes, and criminals arraigned before them, while life was suspended upon a breath, in the courts of England; I have witnessed a Congress in solemn session to give laws to nations; I have tried to conceive of kings, of royal courts, of thrones, and crowns; and of emperors assembled to decide the fate of kingdoms, but dignity and majesty have I seen but once, as it stood in chains at midnight, in a dungeon, in an obscure village of Missouri."[10]

Joseph Smith's display of indignation revealed his character to all those in that wretched prison—similar to the manner in which Christ drove out the money changers in the temple—and Joseph's courage in commanding submission literally silenced the coarse speech of the guards. And to think—he was the one in chains!

In these defining moments, both Anna De Ruyter and Joseph Smith demonstrated tremendous courage and character in the face of hardship and persecution.

True greatness

In his article, "What is True Greatness?" President Howard W. Hunter taught:

"What are the things God has ordained to be 'the common lot of all mankind'? Surely they include the things that must be done in order to be a good father or a good mother, a good son or a good daughter, a good student or a good roommate or a good neighbor.

"Giving consistent effort in the little things in day-to-day life leads to true greatness. Specifically, it is the thousands of little deeds and tasks of service and sacrifice that constitute the giving, or losing, of one's life for others and for the Lord. They include gaining knowledge of our Father in Heaven and the gospel. They also include bringing others into the faith and fellowship of his kingdom."[11]

While these commonplace acts do not usually receive the attention or the adulation of the world, when combined together, these behaviors constitute everyday greatness and help form a person's character.

Not long ago, my husband and I watched a movie produced by a Latter-day Saint filmmaker entitled *One Good Man*. This film tells the story of an ordinary member of the Church, who is called to be the Bishop of his ward. In addition to his Church responsibilities, he is the father of six children, a busy employer, and a conscientious citizen. While watching this film, we were both inspired by the "seeming" ordinariness of this man's life juxtaposed by the goodness of his character. To our minds, this individual exemplifies the vast majority of members of the Church, who like the Savior, "[go] about doing good" (Acts 10:38) and illustrates what primary greatness is all about.

As the only perfect person to have ever lived, Jesus Christ is our Exemplar. Though "the greatest of all" (D&C 19:18), He suffered and sacrificed to fulfill the Father's Plan because of His love for each of us. President David O. McKay taught:

"That man is most truly *great* who is most Christ like. What you sincerely think in your heart of [Jesus] Christ will determine what you are, [and] will largely determine what your acts will be.

"By choosing Him as our ideal, we create within ourselves a desire to be like Him, and to have fellowship with Him. If you think about Him long enough, you will begin to act like Him, and if you act like Him long enough, you will truly become like Him."[12]

Serving and loving our fellow man, showing courage and character in defining moments, and giving consistent effort in the routines of day-to-day life, help us become as He is, and ultimately leads to true greatness.

Initiatives to consider

1. What is your definition of greatness? Which qualities do you admire in "great" individuals?
2. Think of defining moments in your life, which called for courage and character. How did you respond to these challenges?
3. How can you find meaning and purpose in serving those around you while carrying out your daily responsibilities?

[1] Ezra T. Benson, *Teachings of Ezra Taft Benson* (Bookcraft, 1988), 602–604.

[2] *Ibid.*

[3] Spencer W. Kimball, "President Kimball Speaks Out on Service to Others," *New Era*, March 1981.

[4] David McCullough, *The American Spirit* (Simon & Schuster, 2017), 58.

[5] Stephen R. Covey, *Seven Habits of Highly Effective People* (Simon & Schuster, 1989), 30.

[6] Sean Covey, *Fourth Down and Life to Go: How to Turn Life's Setbacks into Triumphs* (Bookcraft, 1990), 61.

[7] Neal A. Maxwell, "Overcome . . . Even as I Also Overcame," *Ensign*, May 1987.

[8] Kitty de Ruyter-Bons, *As I Have Loved You* (Covenant, 2003), 58.

[9] *Ibid*, 62-63.

[10] Parley P. Pratt, *Journal History of the Church of Jesus Christ of Latter-day Saints*, Nov. 7, 1853, 1.

[11] Howard W. Hunter, "What is True Greatness?," *Ensign*, Sept. 1987.

[12] David O. McKay, qtd. in Gene R. Cook, "Charity: Perfect and Everlasting Love," *Ensign*, May 2002.

Chapter 8
Consecration

True success in this life comes in consecrating our lives—
that is, our time and choices—to God's purposes.
> — *D. Todd Christofferson, "Reflections on a*
> *Consecrated Life," Liahona*

In September 2013, the Church-affiliated Polynesian Cultural Center (PCC) commemorated the 50th anniversary of its formation. My husband and I were in Laie, Hawaii, to celebrate our wedding anniversary during this significant milestone, and we spent a full day at the PCC—exploring the Polynesian villages, watching the canoe pageant, and taking in the inspirational night show.

We also visited the BYU-Hawaii campus where we came across the statue of George Q. Cannon and Jonathan Napela, the native Hawaiian convert who helped Elder Cannon translate the *Book of Mormon* into the Hawaiian language.

If ever there were a model of a consecrated person, Jonathan Napela would be it. A native Hawaiian, born an *a'lii* (of chiefly rank) on the island of Maui, and educated at Lahainaluna (a prestigious seminary in Lahaina), Napela was an appointed judge who held a preeminent standing in his community.

The missionaries had had little success teaching the gospel in Maui before Elder George Q. Cannon felt impressed to travel north along the rugged coastline to Wailuku where he sensed that he would find friends who were awaiting him.

Elder Cannon was divinely led to the home of Jonathan Napela, a Christian who had embraced the Protestant faith. Educated, distinguished, a wealthy landowner, and a man of position and influence, Napela immediately recognized the truth of the restored gospel, similar to the way the congregants of the United Brotherhood directly accepted Elder Wilford Woodruff's teachings in Herefordshire, England, in 1840.

Elder George Q. Cannon baptized Jonathan Napela on January 5, 1852. Not long afterwards, Jonathan lost his judgeship due to persecution. The Napela's Protestant minister and other influential Hawaiians tried to persuade them to abandon their association with the Mormon Elders and their teachings, but without success. To Elder Cannon's joy, Jonathan and Kitty Napela stayed faithful to their belief in the doctrines of the Church, although it is not clear if Kitty was ever baptized.

Jonathan Napela had been richly blessed with spiritual gifts, and he participated in a number of remarkable priesthood administrations and manifestations of the Spirit. His influence served as the impetus in advancing the gospel among the Hawaiian people.

By April 1852, Church membership in the islands was estimated at 700, and at the first conference of the

Sandwich Islands Mission, it was announced that Elder Cannon and Brother Napela had commenced work on the translation of the *Book of Mormon* into Hawaiian.

Fifteen months later, the translation was complete, and by 1855, 2000 copies were printed in California. To have the *Book of Mormon* accessible in the Hawaiian language was a great blessing to the missionaries and to the Hawaiian Saints.[1]

Jonathan Napela's role in the establishment of the Church in Hawaii is an inspiring example of consecration, which, by definition means to set apart, or dedicate to a sacred purpose.

Brother Napela paid a high price for his membership, and lost all that he had materially possessed, i.e., his wealth, standing, reputation, and livelihood, yet he remained valiant in his testimony of Jesus and in His restored gospel. Once baptized, he wholeheartedly devoted his intellect, talents, personality, and testimony to the building up of the kingdom of God on the earth.

Render to God all that you have and are

In reminding his people about their eternal indebtedness to God, King Benjamin admonished them "to render to Him all that you have and are" (Mosiah 2: 34). To me this means we give our heart, might, mind, and strength—our personality, our time and talents; in other words, *the very essence of who we are*, to the Lord as an offering in righteousness. In turn, He uses us as instruments in His hand to bless His other children and to bring about His eternal purposes (see Moses 1:39).

Elder Boyd K. Packer explained this concept further:

"We are a covenant people. We covenant to give of our resources in time and money and talent—all we are and all we possess—to the interest of the kingdom of God upon the earth. In simple terms, we covenant to do good."[2]

Although we have not been asked to live the temporal law of consecration at present, we need not wait for a future day to consecrate our lives to the Lord. Elder Neal A. Maxwell put it this way: "We tend to think of consecration only as yielding up, when divinely directed, our material possessions. But ultimate consecration is the yielding up of oneself to God. Heart, soul, and mind were the encompassing words of Christ in describing the first commandment . . ."[3]

In essence, consecration is the law God gives to His covenant people. Striving to live in harmony with this law directly influences who we are, how we act, and the way we present ourselves.

Carole M. Stephens, former First Counselor in the General Relief Society Presidency, summed it up nicely:

"Elder Robert D. Hales taught, 'When we make and keep covenants, we are coming out of the world and into the kingdom of God.'

"We are changed. We look different, and we act different. The things we listen to and read and say are different, and what we wear is different because we become daughters of God bound to Him by covenant."[4]

As we consecrate ourselves to His purposes, our faith in Jesus Christ and in His Atonement will increase, and we can be made holy through Him.

The sacrifice of all things

Our son Colin learned about (the lack of) consecration in dealing with one of his investigators who backed out of a baptismal commitment at the last minute. He and his companion had been working with Brother Ding for some time, and he had made good progress. Then, on the date he was to be baptized, Colin sent this disappointing letter:

"Nana got baptized, but Brother Ding didn't make it . . . That hurt like the dickens! Brother Ding was all set up for his baptismal interview with the Mission President, and he waited and waited, but he did not show!

"When we finally got in touch with Brother Ding, he said that he had recently found a girlfriend and she told him to stop going against the Taiwanese religion. So, he listened to her, and decided he liked Buddhism better because it didn't require anything of him.

"We could hardly believe it. How could he deny all of the feelings and answers he had received through his scripture reading and prayer? We went to his house and saw that he was smoking again, which broke our hearts, since he had previously given it up with God's help. Then he told us that he did not want to get baptized after all. It was so difficult to see someone change so much for the better, and then reject the enabling power of the Atonement."

It is telling to note that this investigator wished to go back to his previous religion "because it did not require anything of him." This is why the Prophet Joseph Smith stated in the *Lectures on Faith* that "a religion that does not require the sacrifice of all things never has power sufficient to produce the faith necessary unto life and salvation."[5]

Being a member of the Church of Jesus Christ of Latter-day Saints *does* require something of us. In fact, it demands our whole souls: "[C]ome unto Christ, who is the Holy One of Israel, and partake of his salvation, and the power of his redemption. Yea, come unto him, and *offer your whole souls as an offering unto him*, and continue in fasting and praying, and endure to the end; and as the Lord liveth ye will be saved" (Omni 1:26). Salvation is not cheap, but rather, dear, as Paul reminds: "[We] are bought with a price" (1 Cor. 7:23).

On Christmas Eve of 1776, General George Washington read a stirring essay, written by Thomas Paine, to his troops. These soldiers had enlisted for only a certain amount of time, and their commission was due to expire. They were cold, miserable, and beaten, and many had lost their motivation to fight. Washington wished to awaken within them the realization that the price of freedom is high and requires great sacrifice.

In his essay, Paine expressed this truism: "What we obtain too cheaply we esteem too lightly; it is dearness only that gives everything its value. Heaven knows how to put a proper price upon its goods."[6] Paine's essay had the desired effect upon Washington's troops, and most of the men reenlisted—pledging their whole souls in the fight for independence.

As I have pondered upon this concept, I feel such admiration for the faith exhibited by the early members of the Church, and by those converts of today who are willing to sacrifice *all* for the sake of the truth. Not to be forgotten are the long-standing members of the Church who day-in and day-out willingly give of their time, talents, and resources to the building up of the Lord's kingdom. To me, these individuals epitomize the consecrated life.

A Visual Testimony

A few years ago, I went to an incredibly inspiring exhibit hosted by the BYU Museum of Art entitled "Minerva Teichert's *Book of Mormon* Paintings." Many members of the Church would recognize Minerva's artwork, although they may not be familiar with her name. A few of my favorite paintings of hers include *Christ in His Red Robe*, *Look to Your Children*, *Queen Esther*, and *Rescue of the Lost Lamb*, among others.

At the exhibit, I was fascinated to learn that to Minerva Teichert (1888-1976), painting was more than just a profession. It was a divine calling—a mission she felt compelled to work on every day. Minerva was a deeply spiritual woman who relied on the Spirit for artistic inspiration. She never started a painting without praying first and "consecrating [her] performance unto [the Lord]" (see 2 Ne. 32:9).

Growing up in Utah and Idaho, Minerva displayed a talent for art from an early age, which her parents encouraged by enrolling her in art lessons as a teenager. After graduating from high school and teaching in rural elementary schools for several years, she moved back East to pursue further art education. She studied at the Art Institute of Chicago and the Art Students League in New York City, becoming one of the few Western women in the early twentieth century to receive formal art training.

While studying in New York City, one particular teacher, an American artist named Robert Henri, recognized Minerva as one of his best students. Henri encouraged her to paint "the Mormon story." Minerva recounts an exchange with him that significantly influenced the course of her artistic life:

"One day he said to me: 'Has anyone ever painted that great Mormon story of yours?'"

"Not to suit me," Minerva responded.

"Well good heavens, girl, what a chance! You have the greatest things on earth to paint. You do it. That's your birthright," Henri encouraged.

"I felt I had been commissioned!" Minerva quipped.

After completing her training, Minerva returned to the West, married Herman Teichert, and raised five children on a ranch in Cokeville, Wyoming, all the while continuing her artistic pursuits. She balanced her responsibilities as wife, mother, rancher, and painter seamlessly, as these roles were all essential elements of her daily life. Her living room became her studio. Her husband, her children, and her neighbors became her models.

Driven to paint, she worked tirelessly for six decades, creating hundreds of portraits and landscapes, chronicles of the Mormon westward movement, murals for the Manti Temple, and the inspiring series of the *Book of Mormon* illustrations.

Minerva was deeply committed to fulfilling Robert Henri's counsel to tell the Mormon story: "We must paint the great story of our pioneers. This story thrills me—fills me—drives me on. We need to make a great American art—to develop a style distinctly our own." She considered these projects as some of the most rewarding experiences of her life.

Although she had not been commissioned to paint

scenes from the *Book of Mormon*, Minerva felt compelled by a sense of mission and purpose to do so. When pressed for her motive, she simply stated: "Because I believe in it." In 1969, she donated the complete set of 42 paintings in the *Book of Mormon* series to BYU.

Minerva's most deeply felt convictions were brought to life in paint. Her remarkable lifetime of artistic consecration is best summarized in her own words: "I have a testimony of the Gospel. Goodness, it is the first thing in my life."[7]

For God? . . . Of course!

When our son, Covey, was serving as a missionary in Richmond Hill, Canada, he found and taught a woman from the Philippines who was living in Canada as a domestic worker. Already a Christian, Sarah had such a pure heart and genuinely desired to do what God would have her do. She immediately accepted the truth of the restored gospel as taught by the Elders.

Generally, when teaching the lesson on the commandments, the missionaries would introduce each commandment and commit the investigator to live it. Quite often, investigators were reluctant to agree to such enormous lifestyle changes and would hesitate or push back; but when Covey and his companion taught Sarah, her response was one of faith and obedience.

Each time they introduced a new commandment and committed Sarah to live it, she would respond: "For God? . . . Of course!" Her dedication to our Heavenly Father, and her desire to keep His commandments, was so fervent that she was willing to make any sacrifice to demonstrate her love for Him.

After His own heart

Recently, a sister in my stake, Lynda Wilson, gave a presentation to the women of our stake on "The Atonement and Grace." Her perspective was so fresh and insightful that it gave new meaning to my understanding of what a consecrated life should look like.

Sister Wilson told about when her husband, Larry, was turning 60 and how she wanted to put on a big celebration for their family and friends. Since her husband's birthday was on New Year's Eve Day, she invited her entire family to stay with them over the Christmas holidays. Between having all their children, complete with spouses and grandchildren living with them, their house was filled to the brim. Lynda described the noise and chaos—toddlers running around, and the TV blasting non-stop, alternating between ESPN and the Hallmark Channel.

Although she was exhausted from the Christmas holidays, Lynda began planning this next event. She noted how she could ask anyone for help, and they would willingly pitch in.

"Could you please take out the garbage?" Lynda would request.

"Happy to help!" someone would respond.

However, a pattern began to take shape. Rather than always having to request assistance, two of the people in that household came alongside Lynda and seemed to anticipate her every need. They felt as she felt. Their desire was to fulfill her desires. They were a man and woman "after her own heart."

One of these individuals spent hours putting together a video presentation on their father's life; the other sat down with Lynda to plan the menu for the dinner, then shopped for the ingredients, and helped prepare the meal. Lynda's panic subsided. She no longer needed to ask for help. She didn't have to go it alone. It became "our" party, not "her" party.

She related that experiencing this "oneness of heart" caused her to contemplate how she interacted with the Lord. She asked herself: *Does He have to ask me for help, or do I sense His needs and respond? Is what is in His heart in my heart too? Am I a woman after His own heart?*

The phrase "a man after mine own heart" means "a kindred spirit" or "someone I can agree with." It originates from two verses in the Bible that explain why the Lord chose David and rejected Saul as the king of Israel:

- "But now thy kingdom shall not continue: the Lord hath sought him *a man after his own heart*" (Sam. 13:14).
- "And when he had removed him, he raised up unto them David to be their king; to whom also he gave testimony, and said, I have found David the son of Jesse, *a man after mine own heart*, which shall fulfill all my will" (Acts 13:22).

This experience fundamentally changed Lynda. She began to recognize that what mattered most was her relationship with God. She wanted Him to be able to count on her. She desired to better know His will, so that He didn't even have to ask for help. She wanted to spiritually progress to the point that what He wanted, she wanted. What He valued, she valued. Sister Wilson taught:

We give our children gifts so they can become

responsible adults. It is the same with God. He gives us gifts so we can eventually 'grow up in Him' and become a person He can trust and work through. He desires for us to become women 'after his own heart.'[8]

Another instance of this depth of consecration is found in the story of the prophet Nephi in the book of Helaman, whose message is rejected again and again by the wicked people of the land. Regardless of their negative response, Nephi continues to preach, and testify, and pray, and have faith in Christ. Finally, the Lord makes this promise to him:

> [B]ecause thou hast done this with such unwearyingness, behold, I will bless thee forever: and I will make thee mighty in faith and in works; yea, even that all things shall be done unto thee according to thy word, for thou shalt not ask that which is contrary to my will (10:5).

Nephi becomes such a trusted disciple that God cannot deny his requests. He has spiritually progressed to the degree that what God desires, Nephi desires. God's will is Nephi's will. Nephi has become "a man after [His] own heart."

In sum, what consecration boils down to is this: cultivating a relationship with God that is after His own heart. When we fully align our will with His and allow His purposes to become ours, we attain this oneness of heart. This level of commitment requires that we "yield to the enticings of the Holy Spirit, and [put] off the natural man and [become] a saint through the Atonement of Christ the Lord" (see Mosiah 3:19). As we do so, He will come to know us, trust us, and enlist us in His service.

Initiatives to consider

1. What does consecration mean to you?
2. What examples do you recognize in those Latter-day Saints around you who have consecrated their lives to God's purposes?
3. How can you more fully become a woman after His own heart?

---

[1] Content taken from *Stewards of the Promise: The Heritage of the Latter-day Saints on the Hawaiian Islands of Maui, Molokai, and Lanai* (1995), ch.1-2.

[2] Boyd K. Packer, *The Holy Temple* (Bookcraft, 1980), 35.

[3] Neal A. Maxwell, "Consecrate Thy Performance," *Liahona,* July 2002, 39.

[4] Carole M. Stephens, "Wide Awake to Our Duties," *Liahona,* Nov. 2012, 115–16.

[5] Joseph Smith, *Lectures on Faith* (Covenant Communications, 2003), 6:7.

[6] Thomas Paine, "The American Crisis," No. 1.

[7] Content taken from "Minerva Teichert's *Book of Mormon* Paintings" exhibit at the BYU Museum of Art.

[8] Lynda Wilson, "The Atonement and Grace," Relief Society Gospel Study Series, 15 Mar. 2018.

Chapter 9
Power

I, Nephi, beheld the power of the Lamb of God, that it descended upon the Saints of the church of the Lamb, and upon the covenant people of the Lord, who were scattered upon all the face of the earth; and they were armed with righteousness and with the power of God in great glory.

— 1 Ne. 14: 14

I was raised in a "household of faith" (D&C 121:45) by parents who devoted their best efforts to gospel teaching, and who gave highest priority to scripture study, prayer, and family home evening. During one particular gospel study session, we settled upon a favorite verse of scripture, which became both a hallmark and a focus for our family:

"Search diligently, pray always, and be believing, and all things shall work together for your good, if ye walk uprightly and remember the covenant wherewith ye have covenanted one with another (D&C 90:24)."

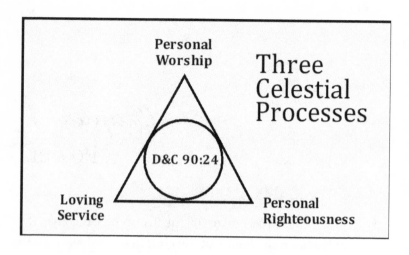

My father called this scripture "the Lord's success formula," and he categorized it into three distinctive parts, which he termed "Celestial processes": personal worship, personal righteousness, and loving service.

PERSONAL WORSHIP: This Celestial process encompasses the first part of the scripture: "Search diligently, pray always, and be believing" (have faith!), as demonstrated through scripture study, prayer, partaking of the sacrament, and temple worship.

Scripture study: "There's power in this book!"

We are all familiar with the song from the *Primary Children's Songbook* entitled, "Scripture Power," but do we ever reflect upon the words of the chorus?

> Scripture power keeps me safe from sin.
> Scripture power is the power to win.

Scripture power! Ev'ryday I need
The power that I get each time I read.[1]

While serving as a missionary in Ireland, I had an experience with an investigator that forever changed my perspective about the power of the *Book of Mormon* to change lives. My companion and I were tracting in Dublin one day when a young man named John Thunder, who was around 22 years old, answered our knock, and allowed us to teach him a first discussion on the doorstep. Although we weren't invited into his home, we gave him a *Book of Mormon* and challenged him to read the verses we had marked.

When we followed up with that young man a few days later, he excitedly invited us into his home and told us what had happened to him in the interim. John explained that after we had left, he placed the *Book of Mormon* on a shelf in his living room, with no intention of reading it. However, every time he entered the room, he felt a compulsion—a spiritual urge—to take it off the shelf and open its pages. He did so. What he discovered in that book was life changing, and by the time we returned he was able to testify: "There's power in this book!"

The *Book of Mormon* was the key to conversion for John Thunder. On the day he was baptized, he wrote a few verses and gave it to my companion and me in an effort to immortalize his testimony of this sacred work:

The *truth* within this book is of God and not of man;
The *love* within this book is of God and not of man;
The *power* within this book is of God and not of man;
I witness the truth, the love, and the power of this book.

During the Sunday morning session of the April 2017

general conference, President Thomas S. Monson implored each of us to "prayerfully study and ponder the *Book of Mormon* each day." He taught: "This morning I speak about the *power* of the *Book of Mormon* and the critical need we have as members of this Church to study, ponder, and apply its teachings in our lives."[2] This was President Monson's final counsel to the Saints before he passed away in January of 2018.

Following up on his invitation during the October 2017 general conference, President Russell M. Nelson noted: "When I think of the *Book of Mormon*, I think of the word *power* . . . Immersing ourselves regularly in the truths of the *Book of Mormon* can be a life-changing experience."[3]

An additional latter-day prophet, President Ezra Taft Benson, used similar words to describe the transformative power found in the *Book of Mormon*:

"It is not just that the *Book of Mormon* teaches us truth, though it indeed does that. It is not just that the *Book of Mormon* bears testimony of Christ, though it indeed does that, too. But there is something more. There is a *power* in the book, which will begin to flow into your lives the moment you begin a serious study of the book. You will find greater *power* to resist temptation. You will find the *power* to avoid deception. You will find the *power* to stay on the strait and narrow path."[4]

A beautiful example of the fulfillment of this promise is found in the life of Elder F. Enzio Busche, a convert to the Church from Dortmund, Germany.

In his autobiography, Elder Busche tells about how he and his wife, Jutta, had been investigating the Church for some time. One of the barriers to their being baptized was Enzio's smoking habit, which began when he was drafted into the German army at the age of 14. At the time he and his wife were taking the missionary discussions, Enzio had been smoking for nearly 12 years, and it seemed impossible for him to overcome this deep-seated habit. Not only did he smoke 40 cigarettes a day, but also, ten small cigars and three to five pipes. Elder Busche remembers being enveloped by smoke at all times.

When their most recent set of missionaries challenged Enzio to quit smoking, his wife joked, "He is good at quitting. He has done it eight times in a row!"[5] Jutta had seen him wrestling with it, and although Enzio knew it was not good to smoke, he did not think he could give it up. This time around, the missionaries encouraged him to ask Heavenly Father for help.

One evening, without telling the missionaries, Enzio knelt to pray and asked God if He would help him quit smoking. At the end of his prayer, he paused to listen as he had been taught to do. The still, small voice of the Spirit penetrated his mind and heart, and whispered, "Yes, I can help you quit smoking, but you have to do something for yourself. Read the *Book of Mormon* in the next thirty days."[6]

Enzio had read the *Book of Mormon* before, but with the intent to disprove and find fault with it. He had not yet read it with a "sincere heart" or with "real intent," as Moroni challenged (see Moroni 10: 3-5). Following the prompting he had received, Enzio divided the *Book of Mormon* into thirty parts, and he made a personal commitment to approach the book with an eye of faith. Little did he know that the cigarette he had smoked prior to offering his prayer that evening was the last one he would ever smoke.

During that period, Enzio was very busy in his professional life, which required him to arise an hour earlier than usual to complete his goal of reading the *Book of Mormon* over a thirty-day span. He remembered: "[W]hen I began to read the *Book of Mormon*, I felt a spirit of strength, comfort, and peace entering my soul."[7]

Three weeks into his experiment, Enzio was right on schedule with his reading goal. He continued to refrain from smoking, and he realized that he was no longer conscious of a desire to smoke. At this point, he finally gained the courage to dispose of all the smoking products in his apartment and to rid them from his life forever. Enzio learned for himself that "when we pray and listen carefully to the promptings of the Spirit, miracles can happen. The things that seem to be too difficult *can* be accomplished."[8]

Indeed, if we allow, the power found in the *Book of Mormon* can literally transform our lives and bring us closer to God. In the words of Joseph Smith: "I told the brethren that the *Book of Mormon* was the most correct of any book on earth, and the keystone of our religion, and a man would get nearer to God by abiding by its precepts, than by any other book."[9] The Prophet Joseph also declared: "Take away the *Book of Mormon* and the revelations, and where is our religion? We have none."[10]

Through the power of the Holy Ghost, which has come upon me countless times while reading the *Book of Mormon*, I can personally witness of its truthfulness.

The power of prayer

One of the sweetest experiences a missionary can have

is to watch an investigator offer a prayer for the very first time. The investigator is often hesitant and unsure, yet so desirous and humble. King Lamoni's father exemplified this meekness of spirit when he prayed: "O God, Aaron hath told me that there is a God; and if there is a God, and if thou art God, wilt thou make thyself known unto me, and I will give away all my sins to know thee" (Alma 22:18).

There is no more reassuring witness of God's love than when we feel His love through prayer. The comforting words of the Primary song ring true:

I feel my Savior's love;
Its gentleness enfolds me,
And when I kneel to pray,
My heart is filled with peace.

He knows I will follow him,
Give all my life to him.
I feel my Savior's love,
The love he freely gives me.[11]

The habit of sincere daily prayer is a recognition and acknowledgement of our utter and complete dependence upon the Lord. There is also a sense of accountability as we address Him by name, seek His will, and ask for His blessings.

Throughout his service as a general authority, President Gordon B. Hinckley encouraged members of the Church "to believe in prayer and the power of prayer." He testified: "Prayer unlocks the powers of heaven in our behalf." He promised: "Be prayerful and the God of heaven will smile upon you and bless you, and give happiness in your hearts and a sense of peace in your lives."[12]

What I have learned, and what I keep learning over and over, is that God has so much light and knowledge He desires to reveal to us, but in order for us to receive it, we need to create an atmosphere in our own personal lives that is conducive to receiving this spiritual enlightenment. "Behold, I stand at the door, and knock: if any man hear my voice, and open the door, I will come in to him, and will sup with him, and he with me" (Rev. 3:20). When we open the door and allow Him into our lives, He will literally pour out His Spirit upon us.

If we qualify, we will grow in this principle of revelation and our spiritual capacity will increase. We will begin to hear the voice of the Spirit more clearly and more frequently, to the point that we shall "know the mysteries and peaceable things—that which bringeth joy, that which bringeth life eternal" (D&C 42: 61).

The sacred emblems of the sacrament

Not long ago, I heard a story about a Latter-day Saint family who was visiting Thailand when the devastating tsunami hit Southeast Asia in December of 2004. The tsunami struck on a Sunday morning, and though on vacation, this family had left their seaside resort to attend their church meetings. The chapel was located on higher ground closer to the mountains, which took them as far away as possible from the destructive waves. Their desire to be with the Saints and to partake of the sacrament literally saved their lives both temporally and spiritually.

The bread and water we partake of during the

sacrament is intended to become part of our very being and to serve as a reminder that we must incorporate His character and reflect His countenance: "I will put my law in their inward parts, and write it in their hearts; and [I] will be their God, and they shall be my people" (Jeremiah 31:33).

Elder D. Todd Christofferson has examined the symbolic nature of the sacramental emblems and the power found in this essential ordinance:

"The symbolism of the sacrament of the Lord's Supper is beautiful to contemplate. The bread and water represent the flesh and blood of Him who is the Bread of Life and the Living Water, poignantly reminding us of the price He paid to redeem us . . . As we drink the water, we think of the blood He shed in Gethsemane and on the cross and its sanctifying power.

"But figuratively eating His flesh and drinking His blood has a further meaning, and that is to internalize the qualities and character of Christ, putting off the natural man and becoming Saints "through the atonement of Christ the Lord" [Mos. 3:19]."[13]

The more gratitude I feel for the Atonement and the love Jesus offers me, the more I value partaking of the sacrament each week. During those times when I am unable to attend sacrament meeting, whether due to sickness or travel, I feel a tremendous void until I can get back to the sacrament table the next Sunday. Without exaggeration, I actually feel an absence of power in my life when I cannot partake of these sacred emblems.

Never pass up an opportunity to partake of the sacrament—for it is the most important event we take part in all week. This essential ordinance spiritually fortifies us and brings power into our lives. Each Sunday, we covenant to do better, to be better, and to take upon ourselves His name. In return, the Lord promises, "that [we] may always have his Spirit to be with [us]" (D&C 20:77)—in essence, He will be by our side. We are in daily need of these blessings.

Temple worship

One of my brothers does something for a living that is extremely difficult for him and is not inherently within his nature. Yet, he feels such a sense of mission about his work, that he pursues it regardless. Long ago, he began tapping into the sources of power that are available to each of us spiritually, and he found that by accessing these sources, he could function professionally at a high level.

He recently remarked: "In order to do what I do professionally, I need to be in the temple every week. I rely on the power with which I am endowed to fuel my work, and the Lord has blessed me greatly for my efforts." This weekly temple worship session has been the primary factor in helping my brother succeed in his professional life, and in reality, it has fundamentally enlarged his capacity.

Several years ago, I made a commitment to follow my brother's example to increase the frequency of my temple service and to claim the blessings God had in store for me. I, too, have felt a source of spiritual power come into my life that I had not previously experienced in all of my years of inconsistent temple attendance.

We have been promised by a latter-day prophet that being in the temple regularly will "refine our natures,

A Converted Woman's Voice

sanctify our lives, and make us better men and women."[14]

A revelation given in the Doctrine and Covenants explains how this happens. "Therefore, in the ordinances thereof, the power of godliness is manifest. And without the ordinances thereof, and the authority of the priesthood, the power of godliness is not manifest unto men in the flesh" (84:20-21).

In regard to this scripture, my parents taught me that participating in the ordinances of the gospel is similar to having a funnel placed upon the top of my head while the powers of godliness are literally poured into my very being. My understanding is that one way we become like God is by becoming "partakers of His divine nature" (see 2 Peter 1:4) through ordinances.

President Lorenzo Snow actually taught: "Participating in the temple ceremonies is the only way that the knowledge locked in one's spirit can become part of one's flesh."[15] As the full power of the gospel of Jesus Christ is found in the Lord's house, who wouldn't wish for the presence of this sanctifying element to change and hallow us?

President Boyd K. Packer issued the following invitation to the membership of the Church: "Come, and claim your blessings."[16]

PERSONAL RIGHTEOUSNESS: This Celestial process is best represented by the phrase in the scripture verse, "If ye walk uprightly . . ."(D&C 90:24). God has given His children *personal* commandments through the Holy Ghost and *general* commandments through His prophets and the scriptures. Our aim is to be obedient to both.

Obedience to personal and general commandments

To qualify for the promised blessings of the Atonement, God has given us commandments, ordinances, and covenants. As we obey these directives, He will bestow His power upon us, and His mercy and grace. I love the insight offered by President Ezra Taft Benson about the principle of obedience: "When obedience ceases to be an irritant and [instead] becomes our quest, in that moment God will endow us with power."[17]

In a landmark general conference talk, Elder Dallin H. Oaks identified two sources of communication that we have with our Heavenly Father—the personal line and the priesthood line. He taught:

"This personal line of communication with our Heavenly Father through His Holy Spirit is the source of our testimony of truth, of our knowledge, and of our personal guidance from a loving Heavenly Father. It is an essential feature of His marvelous gospel plan, which allows each one of His children to receive a personal witness of its truth."[18]

Our family had an experience with this personal line of communication soon after President Thomas S. Monson passed away and before President Russell M. Nelson had been ordained and set apart as the new Prophet. We attended a sacrament meeting where President Nelson was present. The moment he walked through the door, the congregation arose, and the Spirit of the Lord was poured out in abundance.

When seated on the stand, President Nelson gazed out over the congregation as if to "behold us" (see Mark 10:21). His countenance literally radiated goodness and charity—

the pure love of Christ.

Two of our daughters, Megan and Christine, were sitting near the first few rows of the chapel, and both began to cry. Afterwards, they explained that they had received a witness from the Holy Ghost of President Nelson's prophetic calling, and they could not hold back their tears. When asked recently how she felt about President Nelson, Megan testified: "I know he is a prophet. I love him."

The second line of communication is the priesthood line, which is representative of the general commandments. Of this source, Elder Oaks explained:

"The priesthood line is the channel by which God has spoken to His children through the scriptures in times past. And it is this line through which He currently speaks through the teachings and counsel of living prophets and apostles and other inspired leaders. His Church is the way and His priesthood is the power through which we are privileged to participate in those cooperative activities that are essential to accomplishing the Lord's work."[19]

The priesthood line is essential to our growth and development as we cannot be exalted without making covenants and participating in ordinances through divine authority. Jesus Christ established His Church, His priesthood, and His prophet-leaders to administer these ordinances and programs.

To fulfill His divine purposes (see Moses 1:39), both lines of communication are necessary and vital to our spiritual progress. Each of us must obtain a testimony of truth and receive personal revelation for our lives through the Holy Ghost. Correspondingly, the Church functions through divine authority under the direction of those who hold the appropriate priesthood keys. Elder Oaks summed up: "The restored gospel teaches both, and the restored Church provides both."[20]

LOVING SERVICE (to both the living and the dead): The third Celestial process highlights the last part of the scripture found in Doctrine and Covenants 90:24, to "remember the covenant wherewith ye have covenanted one with another."

The covenant we made at baptism as taught by Alma at the Waters of Mormon, includes the willingness "to mourn with those that mourn; yea, and comfort those that stand in need of comfort, and to stand as a witness of God at all times and in all things, and in all places that ye may be in" (Mosiah 18:9). In essence, as baptized members of the Church, we promise to minister to one another and to magnify our callings in missionary, temple, and family history work.

Missionary, temple, and family history work

The most significant duties and responsibilities God requires of His children are to preach the gospel and to seek after our dead. These divinely appointed responsibilities are being fulfilled through the work of the Church today. The number of missionaries and participation in temple and family history work has significantly increased over the past several years. These duties are complementary and interrelated in that they are both an integral part of the work of salvation.

On Easter Sunday, April 3, 1836, the Lord appeared "in a magnificent vision" to Joseph Smith and Oliver Cowdery to accept the Kirtland Temple, one week after it had been dedicated. On that sacred occasion, Moses, Elias, and Elijah also appeared for the purpose of restoring the priesthood keys necessary to gather Israel, seal families together, and prepare the world for the Second Coming of the Savior.

In a general conference address, Elder Quentin L. Cook explained that three executive councils have been established at Church headquarters to oversee and direct these keys and responsibilities: namely, the Missionary Executive Council, the Priesthood and Family Executive Council, and the Temple and Family History Council. He cautioned that, as individuals, "We would all do well to evaluate our effort in pursuing missionary, temple and family history work, and preparing to meet God."[21]

Several years ago, Elder David A. Bednar challenged the rising generation "to learn about and experience the Spirit of Elijah."[22] He promised the youth great blessings as they did so.

Our youngest daughter, Megan, has responded to this invitation. She drives the temple and family history work in our family. She seeks out the names and ordinances needed to be done for our ancestors, and then prints out and distributes the ordinance cards to each family member. She has found great fulfillment—even spiritual *power*—in this work as these responsibilities are a vital part of the work of salvation, not only for the youth but also for the general membership of the Church.

Elder Bednar has taught: "The Lord's work is one majestic work focused upon hearts that change and turn, on sacred covenants, and upon the *power of godliness* manifested through priesthood ordinances."[23]

Keep on the covenant path

On January 16, 2018, the new leadership of the Church was introduced at a press conference, following the passing of President Thomas S. Monson. Speaking from the Salt Lake Temple, new Church President, Russell M. Nelson, addressed each member of the Church, and implored:

"Keep on the covenant path. Your commitment to follow the Savior by making covenants with Him and then keeping those covenants will open the door to every spiritual blessing and privilege available to men, women, and children everywhere . . .

"The end for which each of us strives is to be *endowed with power* in a house of the Lord, sealed as families, faithful to covenants made in a temple that qualify us for the greatest gift of God, that of eternal life. The ordinances of the temple and the covenants you make there are key to strengthening your life, your marriage and family, and your ability to resist the attacks of the adversary. Your worship in the temple and your service there for your ancestors will bless you with increased personal revelation and peace and will fortify your commitment to stay on the covenant path."[24]

Such inspired leadership from our new prophet was a call to each of us to recommit ourselves to the Lord's purposes (see Moses 1:39), and to focus our lives on what matters most. I love the counsel, "Never let things which matter most be at the mercy of things which matter least."[25]

Making our covenants, our families, our consecrated service, and our relationship to God of primary importance is key to living a consecrated life and staying on the covenant path. Lasting joy is found only in being obedient to His commandments and aligning ourselves with His divine purposes.

"All things shall work together for your good"

To sum up the principles taught in this chapter, it is vital to note that as we engage in these three Celestial processes—personal worship, personal righteousness, and loving service—God's divine power will sanctify us, His Spirit will enlighten us, and "all things shall work together for [our] good" (D&C 90:24). What nobler outcome could we possibly desire for our lives?

Initiatives to consider

1) Review the three Celestial processes: personal worship, personal righteousness, and loving service. Explain to a family member what each process means and how they interrelate.

2) Ponder the statement: "Spiritual strength is the natural result of spiritual labor" (Joseph F. McConkie). What essential habits must you develop to maintain spiritual power?

3) Follow Elder Cook's counsel and evaluate your efforts in pursuing missionary, temple and family history work, and preparing to meet God.

---

[1] Clive Romney, "Scripture Power," *The Friend*, Oct. 1987.
[2] Thomas S. Monson, "The Power of the Book of Mormon," *Ensign*, May 2017.

[3] Russell M. Nelson, "The Book of Mormon: What Would Your Life Be Like Without It?," *Ensign*, Nov. 2017.

[4] Ezra T. Benson, "The Book of Mormon—Keystone of Our Religion," *Ensign*, Nov. 1986.

[5] Enzio F. Busche, *Yearning for the Living God* (Deseret Book, 2004), 81.

[6] *Ibid*, 81.

[7] *Ibid*, 82.

[8] *Ibid*, 82.

[9] Joseph Smith, *History of the Church*, 4:461.

[10] Joseph Smith, *Teachings of Presidents of the Church: Joseph Smith* (The Church of Jesus Christ of Latter-day Saints, 2007), 196.

[11] Ralph Rodgers Jr., K. Newell Dayley, Laurie Huffman, "I Feel My Savior's Love," *Children's Songbook* (The Church of Jesus Christ of Latter-day Saints, 1989), no. 74.

[12] Gordon B. Hinckley, *Teachings of the Presidents of the Church: Gordon B. Hinckley* (The Church of Jesus Christ of Latter-day Saints, 2016), 108-109.

[13] D. Todd Christofferson, "The Living Bread that Came Down from Heaven," *Ensign*, Nov. 2017.

[14] Gordon B. Hinckley, "Closing Remarks," *Ensign*, Nov. 2004.

[15] Truman Madsen, *The Temple: Where Heaven Meets Earth* (Deseret Book, 2008), 9-10.

[16] Boyd K. Packer, *Preparing to Enter the Holy Temple* (The Church of Jesus Christ of Latter-day Saints, 2002), 37.

[17] Ezra T. Benson, qtd. in Donald L. Staheli, "Obedience—Life's Great Challenge," *Ensign*, Apr. 1998.

[18] Dallin H. Oaks, "Two Lines of Communication," *Ensign*, Nov. 2010.

[19] *Ibid.*

[20] *Ibid.*

[21] Quentin L. Cook, "Prepare to Meet God," *Ensign*, May 2018.

[22] David A. Bednar, "The Hearts of the Children Shall Turn," *Ensign*, Nov. 2011.

[23] David A. Bednar, "Missionary, Family History, and Temple Work," *Ensign*, Oct. 2014.

[24] Russell M. Nelson, "A Message from the First Presidency," *Church News*, 16 Jan. 2018.

[25] Marion D. Hanks, qtd. in Quinn G. McKay, "Principles in Conflict," *Ensign*, Jan. 1971.

Chapter 10
Inspiration

The Lord has more in mind for you than you have in mind for yourself! You have been reserved and preserved for this time and place. You can do hard things. At the same time, as you love Him and keep His commandments, great rewards—even unimaginable achievements—may be yours.

— President Russell M. Nelson, "You Can Accomplish the Impossible!" New Era, Mar. 2018

Whenever I feel discouraged or discontent, I like to reflect upon the three eternal truths that affirm my infinite worth and give me purpose and meaning:

1) My identity as a beloved daughter of my Heavenly Father.

2) My knowledge that I am of the house of Israel—with all of the marvelous blessings that accompany this birthright.

3) My understanding that I have been reserved to come forth in this last dispensation to fulfill a divine destiny.

I was in a meeting once when Sheri Dew, former Second Counselor in the Relief Society General Presidency, challenged her audience to study D&C 138:55-56 and Abraham 3:22-23, and to ask our Heavenly Father how these scriptures about "the noble and great ones," whom God prepared before the foundation of the world, applied to us. She promised that as we prayerfully pondered these verses, the Spirit would witness to our souls that *we* are the ones the Lord was referring to.

- "I observed that they were also among *the noble and great ones* who were chosen in the beginning to be rulers in the Church of God. Even before they were born, they, with many others, received their first lessons in the world of spirits and were prepared to come forth in the due time of the Lord to labor in his vineyard for the salvation of the souls of men" (D&C 138:55-56).

- "Now the Lord had shown unto me, Abraham, the intelligences that were organized before the world was; and among all these there were many of *the noble and great ones*;

"And God saw these souls that they were good, and he stood in the midst of them, and he said: These I will make my rulers; for he stood among those that were spirits, and he saw that they were good; and he said unto me: Abraham, thou art one of them; thou wast chosen before thou wast born" (Abraham 3:22-23).

These scriptures are incredibly powerful and give us an understanding of the valiant spirits who were reserved to come forth in these latter days. Concerning this foreordination, President George Q. Cannon has said:

"God has reserved . . . the noblest spirits that he had around him to come forth in this last dispensation, because of the greatness and magnitude of the work to be accomplished . . ." He added that those spirits would "have the courage and determination to face the world and all the powers of the evil one . . . and [to] build up the Zion of our God fearless of all consequences."[1]

President Cannon's description is a depiction of each of us. What a privilege it is to be on the earth at this time and to take part in gathering Israel and preparing the world for the Second Coming of the Savior!

I like to gather quotations from Latter-day Apostles and prophets about our destiny as a people. Below are a couple of my favorites:

- "Latter-day Saints need to remember that those who live now are being called upon to work out our salvation in a special time of intense and immense challenges . . . Though we have rightly applauded our ancestors for their spiritual achievements (and we do not and must not discount them now), those of us who prevail today will have done no small thing. The special spirits who have been reserved to live in this time of challenges, and who overcome, will one day be praised for their stamina by those who pulled handcarts."[2]

- "You have been born at this time for a sacred and glorious purpose. It is not by chance that you have been reserved to come to earth in this last dispensation of the fulness of times. Your birth at this particular time was foreordained in the eternities. You are to be the royal [daughters] of the Lord in the last days."[3]

One way we fulfill this divine destiny is to understand our commission and to comprehend the very real duty that lies before us. To be the "chosen" people of the Lord is not status; rather, it refers to the great responsibilities with which we are charged: to be God's servants and to do His work.

Elder Neal A. Maxwell clarifies: "God gives the picks and shovels to the 'chosen' because they are willing to go to work and get calluses on their hands. They may not be the best or the most capable, but they are the most available."[4] To be up to the task at hand, we must fortify ourselves both spiritually and physically.

Sweet are the uses of adversity

I have a close friend I met in college (I will call her 'Jamie'), who is a tremendous person. She is a natural leader and rises to the position of "president" in nearly every organization with which she's involved. Jamie moved across the country soon after she was married, and we didn't stay in touch. I didn't see her again for many years. Recently, she and her family moved back to our area, and we've picked up our friendship once again.

When reconnecting with Jamie, I noticed that she has become a very different person than she was before. While still extremely competent and confident, there is a depth to her that I had not previously known. As we caught up with each other's lives and families, I learned her story.

Jamie had married someone who was not whom he presented himself to be. By the time she discovered this reality, she was pregnant with their first child. Their lives became one of uncertainty and hardship. As her husband's career was never realized, Jamie often needed to assume the role of breadwinner in addition to fulltime homemaker and mother of six (including a handicapped daughter). When I inquired about her wisdom and sweetness of spirit (she literally radiates goodness!), Jamie quickly acknowledged that it was her difficult circumstances that forced her to dig deep and to rely on the Lord in a very real way.

She fasts nearly every Sunday and has done so for most of her married life. In her heart is a prayer that her circumstances will change; however, the inspiration that came to her several years after following this practice was the Lord's voice gently chiding, "You are the one who must be willing to change." Jamie's meekness allowed her to accept this directive, and she has been much more content with her situation ever since.

She insists that adversity is what has made her and her children strong and resilient. Through decades of trials, Jamie has learned the truth that William Shakespeare wrote about approximately 400 years ago: "Sweet are the uses of adversity."[5]

What I've gleaned from Jamie's story is that through tribulation we are tutored—we gain an education that we can learn in no other way. In a letter to her son, the future US President, John Quincy Adams, Abigail Adams taught this principle: "It is not in the still calm of life . . . that great characters are formed . . . Great necessities call out great virtues."[6]

Through the ebb and flow, we come to realize that we are actually participating in life, not just existing. President Gordon B. Hinckley has acknowledged: "I know it isn't easy. It's discouraging at times, sure. Aren't you glad it isn't just fun all the time? Those valleys and discouragement make more beautiful the peaks of achievement."[7]

My friend, Brad Wilcox, wrote a beautiful book entitled *The Continuous Atonement*. One of the many principles he teaches is that life is filled with ups and downs for the express purpose of refining us, teaching us patience and faith, and helping us rely more on our Savior. He writes:

"I remember as a young schoolteacher (with a large active class) asking my wife, Debi, 'When does life even out? Why does it always feel like a roller coaster with so many highs and lows all in the same day? I wish life would just level out.'

"Being a nurse, Debi replied, 'Brad, when you get hooked up to the heart monitor, you don't want to see a straight line. That's bad news. It's the up and down lines that let you know you are alive.'"[8]

As I look back on my life, I recognize that the times I have felt the closest to my Heavenly Father were during the periods of my greatest need. "In the day of their peace they esteemed lightly my counsel; but, in the day of their trouble, of necessity they feel after me" (D&C 101:8). I have learned that we must rely on the Savior not only when times are tough, but also when the sun is shining!

A willingness to change

Several years ago, Court and Mandi Gubler, the creators of the DIY blog, *Vintage Revivals,* stumbled into a Latter-day Saint Addiction Recovery meeting, feeling like "the most broken humans on the planet." After battling

Court's substance addiction over a long period of time, they had come seeking a miracle.

Because of a willingness to change, Mandi testifies that the Atonement of Jesus Christ healed them. Not only did they successfully *get through* the course, but they now *teach* the course and have done so for many years. As Addiction Recovery Program (ARP) Church service missionaries in St. George, Utah, the couple points out that the difference between this recovery program and others like it is the focus on the spiritual.

Court and Mandi have thoroughly reviewed the ARP manual every 12 weeks for the past eight years, and these doctrines have sunk deeply into their hearts and minds. Mandi shared:

"My favorite line in the whole manual says, 'Because of the love and grace of the Savior, you do not have to be what you have been.' I don't know a soul on earth who doesn't want to be more like Christ or more at peace or have more insight into life. That's the whole 12-step program in one sentence."[9]

What is true for Jamie, Court, and Mandi, also rings true for each of us. The Apostle Paul wrote that we must "work out our own salvation with fear and trembling, for it is God who works in you to will and to act according to his purpose" (Philip. 2:12). Through His enabling power, we *can* change, repent, and become righteous forever.

A principle is only as good as its application. On one occasion, our family was in Israel at the BYU Jerusalem Center for Near Eastern Studies. The director of the program wanted us to understand more about Jesus Christ and the Atonement and what it meant for us in our daily lives.

He took us outside to see the olive press that was there in the garden and pointed out its symbolism. He picked one of the olives from the olive tree and had our brother Sean taste it. It was bitter and repulsive, and Sean quickly spat it out. Then our guide asked us a penetrating question: "How can you take something so bitter as this olive and make it into something as sweet as olive oil?"

He then shared the experience of being in this same spot with one of the Apostles when he was visiting Israel. He asked him the question, "How can you take something so bitter and turn it into something so sweet?" With tears streaming down his face as he contemplated the question, this Apostle answered, "Pressure."

Our guide continued to illustrate: "Isn't it interesting that in Gethsemane, which literally means 'place of the olive press,' the Savior took on the pressure of all the world and of all its sins? Because of that Atonement, He can take a heart that is bitter and turn it into something sweet. He can transform a person who is broken into someone whole."

Our family has never forgotten that experience when we learned that even the most bitter and tasteless of us can be redeemed by our Savior, Jesus Christ, and transformed into something beautiful.[10]

The process of spiritual growth

In a general conference talk, Elder Lynn G. Robbins offered the following perspective as to why God allows us to struggle and stumble in our attempts to improve:

- First, the Lord knows that "these things shall give [us] experience and shall be for [our] good" (D&C

122:7).

- Second, to allow us to "taste the bitter, that [we] may know to prize the good" (Moses 6:55).

- Third, to prove that "the battle is the Lord's" (1 Sam. 17:47), and it is only "by His grace" that we can accomplish His work and become like Him (Jacob 4:7).

- Fourth, to help us develop and hone scores of Christ-like attributes that cannot be refined except through opposition and "in the furnace of affliction" [Isaiah 48:10].[11]

When we rise each time we fall, we show a willingness to grow and to progress and to lean upon the Lord for assistance—for it is through our weakness that God can work miracles. Line upon line, step by step, little by little, we become more like Him. He reassures, "My grace is sufficient for thee: for my strength is made perfect in weakness (2 Cor.12:9).

To my dream girl

When Ann Madsen was thirteen years old, she accepted a challenge to read the *Book of Mormon*. One night, quite late, Ann finished reading its pages, and knelt down to ask God "if these things [were] not true," as Moroni encouraged (see Moroni 10:4)— fully expecting an answer to her prayer. With real intent, having faith in Christ, she felt the Spirit testify to her in a dramatic way that the book *was* true.

Not long after, Ann and a close friend hiked to the top of Little Mountain near Salt Lake City to discuss their hopes and dreams. They went fasting. While there, they set lofty goals about what they wanted to have happen in their lives. The more they talked, the more serious they became about achieving these aspirations, and they consecrated themselves to God and his purposes.

They carefully wrote down these goals. They also determined the kind of person they wanted to marry—one who was true to the gospel and who was spiritually strong. Ann, in particular, made the decision that she would marry a returned missionary in the house of the Lord.

Fast-forward four years. Ann is now seventeen years old, and she reads an inspiring article in *The Improvement Era* (the forerunner to *The New Era*) entitled, "To My Dream Girl," written by "A Recently Returned Missionary." She clips out the article and posts it on the bulletin board in her closet, noticing it nearly every day. It represents the ideal of the young woman she desires to become.

The next time we catch up with Ann, she is a sophomore at the University of Utah. A mutual friend introduces her to Truman Madsen. That very evening, Truman picks up Ann from a church meeting, and takes her up to his favorite spot in the mountains where they look out over the city. They converse easily and openly and discuss what they are each looking for in their future spouse.

When Truman describes the girl of his dreams, Ann replies: "The girl you're describing reminds me of this article I have on the wall in my closet called, 'To My Dream Girl.' If I ever meet the man who wrote that article, I would marry him just like that!" (And she snaps her fingers). Truman just smiles.

After dating for a few years, Truman plans a birthday dinner, complete with a special cake, where he proposes to Ann at the Hotel Utah overlooking the Salt Lake Temple. Truman discloses: "You see, sweetheart, dreams do come true. I am the 'recently returned missionary' who wrote that article."[12]

If ever there were an example of how we become like that which we habitually admire, this would be it. As we set righteous goals, and focus all of our thoughts, feelings, and actions toward fulfilling them, we begin to achieve them. Elder Joseph B. Wirthlin put it this way: "Don't worry about searching for who you are; focus your energies on creating the kind of person you want to be!"[13]

Remember, God has more in mind for us than we have in mind for ourselves. He sees things in us that we do not see in ourselves. Our mission and purpose are divine. We are of the House of Israel, and as such, we are entitled to all of the blessings that have been promised to this lineage. Live for them. They are all predicated upon our ability to live in harmony with His teachings, knowing the mind and the will of the Lord and following His guidance, listening and observing, keeping in tune with all that He has given to direct our lives.

As we petition our Father in Heaven for the inspiration of His Holy Spirit, He will guide and direct us and give us courage to live His commandments and open our eyes to see into the future of our own lives and into the power and possibility in the accomplishment of every righteous desire of our hearts.

Initiatives to consider

1. Ponder on the scriptures and statements about being one of the "noble and great ones" of this dispensation. Allow that knowledge to penetrate your soul and become an integral part of your identity.

2. Why does our Heavenly Father allow us to experience adversity? Identify the hardships you have experienced which have factored into your spiritual growth.

3. How can you focus your energies on creating the kind of person you wish to be?

---

[1] George Q. Cannon, *Gospel Truth: Discourses and Writings of President George Q. Cannon, Vol. 1* (Deseret Book, 1974), 18.

[2] Neal A. Maxwell, *Notwithstanding My Weakness* (Deseret Book, 1981), 18-19.

[3] Ezra T. Benson, "To the Youth of the Noble Birthright," *Ensign*, May 1986.

[4] Neal A. Maxwell, *Deposition of a Disciple* (Deseret Book, 1976), 54.

[5] William Shakespeare, *As You Like It*, Act 2, Scene 1, Line 14.

[6] Abigail Adams, Letter to John Quincy Adams, 19 Jan. 1780.

[7] Gordon B. Hinckley, *Discourses, Volume 1: 1995-1999* (Deseret Book, 2005), 1:301.

[8] Brad R. Wilcox, *The Continuous Atonement* (Deseret Book, 2009), 188.

[9] Sydney Jorgensen, "How St. George Blogging Couple 'Vintage Revivals' Found Healing Through LDS Addiction Recovery," *Deseret News*, 20 Mar. 2018.

[10] Material taken from Maria Covey Cole and Stephen M.R. Covey, "Four Attributes of an Influential Teacher," *Church News*, 20 Nov. 2015.

[11] Lynn G. Robbins, "Until Seventy Times Seven," *Ensign*, May 2018.

[12] Content taken from a personal interview with Ann Madsen, June 2018.

[13] Joseph B. Wirthlin, "Lessons Learned in the Journey of Life," *Ensign*, Dec. 2000.

Chapter 11
Nourishment

I looked on my right hand, and beheld, but there was no man that would know me: refuge failed me; no man cared for my soul.

— Ps. 142:4

Twice a year, our stake holds a Gospel Study Series for the sisters of the Relief Society. This past session, one of the counselors in the stake Relief Society presidency, Stephanie Miner, addressed the topic, "The Atonement and Spiritual Gifts."

Stephanie talked about the time she put up a "dream board" in her closet. It was meant to represent her goals, her ambitions, and her hopes for the future. She created a collage of pictures that represented the things she valued most. She played with it a bit—taking some pictures off and adding other pictures to the board. Over time, it became clear what her highest priorities were.

After a while, Stephanie felt impressed to remove the collage from the dream board in her closet and replace it with a single picture of the Savior and the document, "The

Living Christ." She began looking at these items every day while she dressed and thought about Him while she spiritually prepared for the day.

Around that same time, she began feeling an underlying sense of peace and joy, such as she had never experienced before. It imperceptibly worked its way into her heart and permeated her soul. Stephanie tried to identify the source of this tranquility, and it finally dawned on her that it was her focus on the Savior that had created this sense of well-being.

I find it revealing that it was in Stephanie's "closet" where she came to know and love the Lord, similar to the manner in which Ann Madsen developed into Truman's "dream girl"—for it was in her "closet" where Ann first began to dream.

A person's closet represents intimacy—a safe haven where one may withdraw from the world to renew his or her spirit. The scriptures clearly teach about the sacred nature of creating such a refuge:

- "But thou, when thou prayest, *enter into thy closet,* and when thou hast shut thy door, pray to thy Father which is in secret" (Matt. 6:6).
- "But this is not all; ye must *pour out your souls in your closets,* and your secret places, and in your wilderness" (Alma 34. 26).
- "He went in therefore, and *shut the door upon them* twain, and prayed unto the Lord" (2 Kgs. 4: 33).

A few years ago, during stake conference, the visiting general authority invited the wife of our stake president to bear her testimony. Sister Castillo painted a tender picture of her husband's practice of entering into his "closet" each morning to pray. She told of how she could overhear the sweet sounds of his muffled prayer as he poured out his heart to God. She confided that the good life he led, and his ability to spiritually lead our stake, had its origin in that private place.

Soon after returning from his mission, my nephew, Britain Covey, spoke to our extended family about some of the insights he had learned while serving. Drawing upon an intense study of the scriptures, Brit realized that many sacred experiences happened "in the wilderness," where the Lord and His disciples withdrew—to recharge their batteries and receive inspiration. Britain challenged each family member to follow the example of the Savior, and on a regular basis, escape from the world, sacrifice some of our own personal comforts, and create a sanctuary where we may find strength and solace. In other words, to "create our own wilderness."

Many years ago, my father spoke at the BYU Education Week Devotional on the topic, "Never Leave Your Sacred Grove." The premise of his talk was about the importance of revisiting those sacred moments in our lives that define us.

Similar to Joseph Smith, our "sacred grove" experiences are revelatory—such as the time the Holy Spirit testified to our spirit of the reality of God and of His Son, the moment we received the spiritual knowledge that the *Book of Mormon* is the word of God, or when the Holy Ghost witnessed to us of the prophetic calling of the President of the Church, or confirmed the truth that the Lord's Church has been restored to the earth.

Spiritual impressions like these require that we take a step back to remember, renew our covenants, and recommit to living our Heavenly Father's Plan. Dad taught:

> "God has ordained certain places to be 'sacred groves'—the private prayer; the sacrament; the temple with its washing and anointing, endowment, and sealing rooms; also, honest moments of meditation, fasting, and scripture reading."[1]

These "sacred grove" experiences are as vital to our spirits as food is to the sustenance of our physical bodies. They endow us with power and with the courage and integrity to be true to what we know to be true.

Whether it be in your *closet*, your *wilderness*, or your *Sacred Grove*, we must never leave our own private sanctuary where we receive the spiritual nourishment and inspiration needed to lift and sustain us.

What do they do for their souls?

As daughters of God, our souls are filled with intelligence, light, and love, and clothed with the Spirit of the Lord. It is our privilege and obligation to nourish our souls and the souls of those children within our stewardship in their daily need.

- "Yea, at that day, will they not receive the strength and nourishment from the true vine?" (1 Ne. 15:15)
- "I am the vine, ye are the branches: He that abideth in me, and I in him, the same bringeth forth much fruit: for without me ye can do nothing" (John 15:5).

Each of us must regularly care for ourselves by nourishing all four dimensions of the human personality: spirit, mind, body, and soul; and then, see to the needs of those within our stewardship.

"Our Heavenly Father placed the responsibility upon parents to see that their children are well fed, well-groomed and clothed, well trained, and well taught. Most parents protect their children with shelter—they tend and care for their diseases, provide clothes for their safety and their comfort, and supply food for their health and growth. *But what do they do for their souls*?"[2]

A careful study of how our Father in Heaven cares for *His* children can help us accomplish this weighty task with our own. The following verse in the *Book of Mormon* highlights the process:

"And after they had been received unto baptism, and were wrought upon and cleansed by the power of the Holy Ghost, they were numbered among the people of the church of Christ; and their names were taken, *that they might be remembered and nourished by the good word of God,* to keep them in the right way, to keep them continually watchful unto prayer, relying alone upon the merits of Christ, who was the author and the finisher of their faith (Moroni 6:4)."

Attending our church meetings, enjoying fellowship with the Saints, and partaking of the sacrament is analogous to consuming "a green smoothie for the soul" (a phrase attributed to Melanie Marcheschi).

Care for our spirits

Being worthy of and qualifying for the Holy Ghost is one of the most important ways we can spiritually nourish our spirits. After we are baptized and confirmed members of the Church of Jesus Christ of Latter-day Saints, we are promised this gift. This is real. The power is there.

President Lorenzo Snow said: "[It} is the grand privilege of every Latter-day Saint . . . to have the manifestations of the spirit every day of our lives."[3] Yet, as Brigham Young pointed out: "[In] this respect, we live far beneath our privileges."[4]

God can assist us with our major problems in life, in every problem, if we seek Him humbly and worthily. He will give us the stimulation and the inspiration and the enlightenment, yes, even knowledge and understanding, so that we will be able to choose wisely and make proper decisions. We will learn our own capacity and go forward in developing the potential that the Lord has blessed us with into the most useful channels that will be helpful to our Father in Heaven in the advancement of His kingdom.

Creating and maintaining righteous routines and holy habits will allow us to be sensitive to these promptings from the Holy Ghost and will keep us in alignment with God's Plan for His children. The Apostle Paul in the New Testament and the Lord in the Doctrine and Covenants talk about fortifying ourselves with spiritual armor: "Put on the whole armor of God" (see Eph. 6:11-18 and D&C 27:15-18). When we study the scriptures and pray, partake of the sacrament, and attend the temple, it's as though we are clothing our spirits with protective armor.

Elder M. Russell Ballard says he likes to compare spiritual armor with chain mail—the dozens of tiny steel links that allow greater movement, yet effectively keep us safe from harm. He explains:

"It has been my experience that there is not one great and grand thing we can do to arm ourselves spiritually. True spiritual power lies in numerous smaller acts woven together in a fabric of spiritual fortification that protects and shields from all evil."[5]

Former General Young Women's President, Sister Elaine Dalton, further clarified: "When you do small things consistently, they become part of who you are, and they change you. It really is 'by small and simple things [that] great things [are] brought to pass'" [Alma 37:6].[6]

Emotional well-being

Mental health is an essential part of one's emotional well-being and must not be forgotten or ignored. Former BYU quarterback, Tanner Mangum, took to Twitter to share his story of depression for Mental Health Awareness Week. He wrote:

"Not many people know that I suffer from mild depression and anxiety. I take antidepressants every day to help with my condition, have visits with a counselor, and I am not ashamed; on the contrary, I am proud to embrace my own personal journey, accept, and love myself—flaws and all.

"This might be surprising to many, due to my normally optimistic, outgoing and happy personality, but I hope that we can understand that just because someone is beaming brightly on the outside doesn't mean they are free from their own personal struggles underneath the surface. We are all human, each with unique battles, and I promise that these battles are better fought together than alone.

"Mental illness is one of my personal battles, and I want to offer my love and support to all those who suffer in one way or another. You are not alone. There is help."[7]

I have close family members with mental health challenges, and they would reiterate Tanner's plea to reach out to others in an effort to nurture the emotional well-being of those who struggle. Elder Jeffrey R. Holland made this clear when he addressed these issues in a beautiful general conference talk:

"However bewildering this all may be, these afflictions are some of the realities of mortal life, and there should be no more shame in acknowledging them than in acknowledging a battle with high blood pressure or the sudden appearance of a malignant tumor . . .

"Though we may feel we are 'like a broken vessel,' as the Psalmist says (Psalm 31:12), we must remember, that vessel is in the hands of the divine potter. Broken minds can be healed just the way broken bones and broken hearts are healed. While God is at work making those repairs, the rest of us can help by being merciful, nonjudgmental, and kind."[8]

As disciples of Jesus Christ, we must heed the teaching of the Apostle Paul, who instructed that we must have "compassion one of another" (1 Peter 3:8). The older I grow, the more deeply I've come to learn that we *all* have our struggles. Some may be more apparent than others, but struggles beneath the surface can be equally as challenging as those that are visible.

Care for our minds

For those who value education and the life of the mind, this insight by President Gordon B. Hinckley rings true: "None of us . . . knows enough. The learning process is an endless process. We must read, we must observe, we must assimilate, and we must ponder that to which we expose our minds."[9]

Legendary UCLA basketball coach, John Wooden, had a lifelong thirst for knowledge that he inherited from his father, Joshua Wooden. When Joshua's children graduated from elementary school, he gave them each a little card on which were inscribed his "Seven Rules for Living." Embedded within the list was this gem: "Drink deeply from good books."[10]

There is no doubt that what we read shapes who we are. In reading, we experience one of the greatest pleasures human life can afford: books sweeten, nourish, brighten, and enrich our lives.

For me, there is an interdependent relationship between reading and writing. In order to write, I need to read. It feeds my soul and inspires me with insights beyond my own. As my freshman English teacher, VerDon Ballantyne, reiterated to our class, day after day, as we studied the great literature of the ages: "Man left in his own experience suffers eternally from an insufficiency of data."

Through literature, we meet characters we would never meet and go places we would never go. "Literature is considered such an important medium—more than television, more than films, [even] more than art—because literature brings us closest to the human heart," writes Jim Trelease, author of *The Read-Aloud Handbook*. This heartfelt, vicarious experience helps us develop a moral intelligence and gain greater wisdom and understanding.

The road to happiness

During the days of the founding of our country, education was seen as the road to happiness. Historian David McCullough points out:

"In that age of the Enlightenment, Washington, Adams, Jefferson each made [this] point, many times. When our founders spoke of the 'pursuit of happiness,' they did not mean long vacations or the piling up of things.

"Happiness was in the enlargement of one's being through the life of the mind and of the spirit. And what was true for the individual was true for a people.

"Everything was of interest and there was virtually nothing that could not be learned through a close study of books. That was the creed. 'I must judge for myself, but how can I judge, how can any man judge, unless his mind has been opened and enlarged by reading,' John Adams wrote as a young man. 'I cannot live without books,' Jefferson famously told Adams in their old age.

"So, read. Read for pleasure. Read to enlarge your life. Read history, read biography, learn from the lives of others."[11]

It is crucial for us and for our families to understand the centrality of reading, the thoughtful discussion of good books, and the cultivation of the moral and intellectual development of each family member.

I am grateful for the home environment my parents created for my siblings and me. This foundation initiated our love for learning and fueled our lifelong passion for literature and the arts. Cultivating an atmosphere in our homes where a love of good literature abounds is one of the most important life experiences we can provide.

Care for our bodies

My mother subscribed to season tickets at the ballet, and I often attended with her. While at Ballet West's "The Shakespeare Suite" recently, I was in awe of the beautiful bodies of the dancers. To me, they represent discipline, precision, and fluidity of movement—exhibiting the body as art form.

Observing the dancers, I was reminded of Martha Graham's description of the sacredness of the body. Martha Graham was an American modern dancer and choreographer (spanning a 70-year period!), and the founder of the internationally acclaimed Martha Graham Dance Company. She wrote: "The body is a sacred garment: it is what you enter life in and what you depart life with, and it should be treated with honour, and with joy and with fear as well. But always, though, with blessing."[12]

Our physical bodies are a stewardship, given to us by a loving Heavenly Father who desires that we honor Him by honoring the bodies which house our spirits.

I love what Elder Harold Hillam expressed about the importance of this principle. He said: "Spiritual well-being is vital, but how you feel physically is also significant."[13] He went on to advocate for the continual need of physical exercise, sufficient sleep, and sound nutrition.

My friend Jody introduced me to a book entitled, *Spark: The Revolutionary Science of Exercise and the Brain,* by John J. Ratey, M.D., which scientifically backs up Elder Hillam's counsel. In this work, Dr. Ratey explores the mind-body connection, maintaining that exercise is our best defense against everything from stress to depression to ADD to addiction to menopause to memory loss. He claims that the evidence is overwhelming: aerobic exercise physically transforms our brains and helps us function at top capacity.

President Boyd K. Packer has taught "that our spirit and our body are combined in such a way that our body becomes an instrument of our mind and the foundation of our character."[14] He makes the point that these elements of one's nature are not separated, but rather, fundamentally intertwined.

Personally, I have found this principle to be true. When I am exercising consistently, getting sufficient rest, and eating healthy, I experience an underlying sense of both physical and spiritual well-being.

Own the morning, own the day

Establishing a morning routine to care for our spirits, minds, and bodies is a vital part of nourishing our souls and helps us build up a reserve of spirit and power. I've heard this daily pattern referred to in a myriad of ways—all similar in meaning and equally efficacious: "daily private victory," "hour of power," the "five firsts," "own the morning; own the day," et alia.

In a recent conversation with my brother, Sean, he told me how essential his "hour of power" has become for him. He acknowledged that he follows through on his morning routine about 80% of the time. When he is on task, Sean does one half hour of exercise, followed by one half hour of scripture study, prayer, and planning. He considers this time to be spiritual, mental, and physical training for the soul in that it clears his mind and compels him to focus on what matters most.

He shared one experience when he returned home late from a stressful day at work only to discover that his wife and daughter had bought a macaw (large tropical parrot) without his knowledge. They already had a houseful of pets, and he was annoyed by the screeching noises of this new one. He said some unkind things to his wife, Rebecca, and went to bed.

The next morning, Sean woke up and did not feel like having his "daily private victory." Regardless, he got up and went through the motions. During that period, he felt prompted to apologize to Rebecca, which he did. He explained that he was so grateful he had made things right because it ended up being one of the most critical days at work in regard to making financial decisions for the company. More than anything, he needed his very best judgment on that particular day. Because Sean had paid the price to nourish his body and soul, his mind was clear, his spirit was free from guilt and pride, and he was able to tap into a higher power.

Take time to be holy

In her book, *What Would a Holy Woman Do?*, Sister Wendy Watson Nelson tells about the time in November 2007, when her husband, President Russell M. Nelson, was to rededicate the temple in Tonga. In preparation for the dedication, President Nelson walked through the newly remodeled temple to make sure everything was in perfect order. He found that it was.

However, upon close inspection, he found that the words, "House of the Lord, Holiness to the Lord," had not been engraved on the outside wall of the temple. Without those words affixed to the temple, it could not be dedicated! The omission was quickly fixed, the words were placed, and the temple in Tonga was rededicated on schedule.

This experience prompted Sister Nelson to begin thinking about the importance of the phrase, "Holiness to the Lord," and the concept of holiness in general. She asked herself: *What do I need to change in my life to have those words—Holiness to the Lord—placed upon my life? And if those words were placed, what would that mean?*

Sister Nelson began experimenting with the question: *What would a holy woman do?* She found that looking at life through this "lens," or frame of reference, completely changed her way of thinking and favorably affected the way she responded to circumstances.[15]

In Doctrine and Covenants 46:33, the Lord commanded us to "practice virtue and holiness before [Him] continually." In anticipation of our "how-to" question, He instructed, "I am able to make you holy" (D&C 60:7).

Sister Carol F. McConkie, former First Counselor in the Young Women General Presidency, encouraged Latter-day Saint sisters to "choose holiness." As a follow up to that invitation, she explained how God can make us holy:

"We recognize the multitude of tests, temptations, and tribulations that could pull us away from all that is virtuous and praiseworthy before God. But our mortal experiences offer us the opportunity to choose holiness. Most often it is the sacrifices we make to keep our covenants that sanctify us and make us holy."[16]

Making the sacrifices necessary to keep our covenants

truly is a sanctifying process. A popular Methodist hymn, entitled "Take Time to Be Holy," reminds us that our focus on holiness must be both persistent and continuous:

> Take time to be holy, the world rushes on;
> Spend much time in secret with Jesus alone.
> By looking to Jesus, like him thou shalt be;
> Thy friends in thy conduct his likeness shall see.[17]

How does the Lord make us holy? What perspective can we adopt, and actions can we take to bring holiness into our lives and make it part of our very beings?

I believe the answer lies in taking the time to nourish our souls on a daily basis. As we do so, we come to know and love the Lord by coming to know His mind and will—through deep meditation and prayer, feasting upon the scriptures, going into our "closet," so to speak, and taking the Holy Spirit for our guide (see D&C 45:57).

Then, when our heart is right and centered on the Savior, we naturally desire to keep His commandments and honor the covenants we have made with Him. "The beauty of holiness" (see Psalm 96:9) is embodied in the cultivation of such a disposition, and ultimately, we become as He is.

Initiatives to consider

1. What does it mean to "enter into your closet"? Where would you consider your sacred retreat to be?

2. Caring for the spirit, mind, body, and soul is essential to a person's well-being. How can you regularly nourish these four dimensions of the

human personality?

3. In such a hectic world, when can you set aside time
   to be holy?

---

[1] Stephen R. Covey, "Never Leave Your Sacred Grove," 6 Jun. 1967.

[2] Spencer W. Kimball, "Train Up a Child," *Ensign*, Apr. 1978.

[3] Lorenzo Snow, *Conference Report,* Apr. 1899, 52.

[4] Brigham Young, *Deseret News Semi-Weekly*, 3 Dec. 1867, 2.

[5] M. Russell Ballard, "Be Strong in The Lord," *Ensign*, July 2004.

[6] Elaine S. Dalton, "Introduction to Personal Progress," *The New Era*, Sept. 2011.

[7] Published in the *Deseret News*, 5 Apr. 2017.

[8] Jeffrey R. Holland, "Like a Broken Vessel," *Ensign*, Nov. 2013.

[9] Gordon B. Hinckley, *Teachings of Gordon B. Hinckley* (Deseret Book, 1997), 298.

[10] Don Yaeger, *A Game Plan for Life: The Power of Mentoring* (Bloomsbury, 2009), 13.

[11] David McCullough, *The American Spirit* (Simon & Schuster, 2017), 101-102.

[12] Martha Graham, *This I Believe: The Personal Philosophies of Remarkable Men and Women,* Vol. 2 (Henry Holt, 2006).

[13] Harold G. Hillam, "Not for the Body," *Ensign*, Oct. 2001.

[14] Boyd K. Packer, "The Instrument of Your Mind and the Foundation of Your Character,"*BYU Speeches*, 2 Feb. 2003.

[15] Wendy W. Nelson, *What Would a Holy Woman Do?* (Deseret Book, 2013), 1-2.

[16] Carol F. McConkie, "The Beauty of Holiness," *Ensign,* May 2017.

[17] William D. Longstaff, *The United Methodist Hymnal* (The United Methodist Publishing House, 1989), no. 395.

Chapter 12
Discipleship

Verily, I say unto you all: Arise and shine forth, That thy light may be a standard for the nations.

— D&C 115:5

Several years ago, I became fascinated with Lehi's Dream in the *Book of Mormon*. This interest began after reading a couple of articles published in Church magazines within a year of one another about how Lehi's Dream pertains to us today.

The first article was taken from a talk given at BYU by President Boyd K. Packer, entitled "Finding Ourselves in Lehi's Dream,"[1] and the second was an article written by Elder David A. Bednar, entitled "Lehi's Dream: Holding Fast to the Rod."[2]

I was particularly captivated by this intriguing statement by President Packer: "You may think that Lehi's dream or vision has no special meaning for you, but it does. You are in it; all of us are in it." He then went on to declare: "Lehi's dream has in it *everything* a Latter-day Saint needs to understand the test of life."

As I pondered President Packer's claim and began to sense the applicability of Lehi's Dream in my own life, my husband Dave and I felt to apply it to our family life as well. We decided to develop a family mission statement based on the concepts taught in this great vision.

We already had a family mission statement we'd selected as parents when our children were very young, but at this stage in our lives we desired to involve the entire family in the process. We wanted to create a family mission statement that would be meaningful to each individual. We realized that to fully engage the children, we needed to take our time, have each family member personally study Lehi's Dream, create opportunities for meaningful discussions around the topic, and allow each person's voice to be heard and valued.

And so, many years ago on Christmas Eve, my husband Dave presented a beautiful family home evening lesson introducing this concept, during which he challenged us to develop a family mission statement based on Lehi's Dream. He gave us three symbolic gifts to begin our initiative: a folder of articles about Lehi's Dream written by Apostles of the Lord; a piece of jewelry symbolizing the Tree of Life—necklaces for the girls, tie pins for the boys; and a framed print of a painting by Annie Henrie of a family kneeling around the Tree of Life while partaking of the fruit, which we hung in our front entry way.

Dave's challenge inspired us, and we determined to come up with a mission statement that would be meaningful for our family.

During the year, we held many discussions during family home evenings around this topic. It was interesting to hear the insights from the children as they read the account in the *Book of Mormon* as to what stood out to them and what they thought we should emphasize in our family mission statement. We circulated a running list of ideas.

As we studied and discussed Lehi's Dream, we began to sense the importance of the rod of iron in leading individuals to the Tree of Life. We came to the conclusion that the iron rod, as interpreted by Nephi, symbolized the word of God, while the Tree of Life represented the love of God, and the fruit of the tree embodied the Atonement of Jesus Christ.

We began to distinguish between the four different groups of people Nephi identified in the interpretation of his father's dream. We learned that the first group consisted of those who got on the path that led to the Tree, but when the mists of darkness (or temptations) arose, they let go of the rod of iron, wandered off, and were lost.

We recognized that the second group consisted of those who got on the path, held on to the rod that led to the Tree, and actually made it to the Tree and partook of the fruit. But it was *after* they partook of the fruit that they became ashamed, due to the laughing and mocking of those who were in the Great and Spacious building, which characterized the Pride of the World.

Of this group, President Packer said: "One word in this dream . . . should have special meaning to young Latter-day Saints. The word is after. It was *after* the people had found the tree that they became ashamed, and because of the mockery of the world they fell away." *These are members of the Church he is referring to!* President Packer continued: "At your baptism and confirmation, you took hold of the iron rod. But you are never safe. It is *after* you have partaken of that fruit that your test will come."[3]

We discovered that the third group of people in Lehi's Dream got on the path that led to the Tree, held fast to the iron rod, made it to the Tree, and partook of the fruit. Elder Bednar noted that the key characteristic of those who pressed forward is that they "continually [held] fast to the rod of iron." These people were also subjected to the laughing and mocking of those in the Great and Spacious building, but the difference was, as Nephi distinguished, "we heeded them not."[4]

We realized that the fourth group of people represented those, who like Laman and Lemuel, never even set foot on the path.

As a family, we determined that we wanted to be like the third group of people who press forward with faith and conviction, continually "holding fast" to the rod of iron, until we too, come forth, fall down, and partake of the fruit of the Tree.

After several months of study, thought, and discussion, we finally narrowed down our family mission statement to two choices. The first option was fashioned by Christine and Colin, which captured what we wanted to say but sounded a little too evangelic when chanted: "Hold tight, take a bite, share the light!" So, we ultimately decided on the second alternative that our oldest son Covey had come up with, which was "Meet at the Tree."

We all felt really good about our selection, "Meet at the Tree," because of what it represented. To us, it implies that we are all on our own spiritual journey. We must each get on the straight and narrow path that leads to the Tree of Life, press forward with steadfastness in Christ, hold fast to the rod of iron, arrive at the Tree, and partake of the fruit. When we do so, we will be eternally united with our family as we kneel in worship of our Savior and partake of the fruit of His Atonement.

On Christmas Eve a year later, Dave prepared another family home evening lesson in an effort to follow up on our experience. He asked us to come prepared to share what our family mission statement meant to each of us, and how we had tried to apply it in our lives. When it was my turn, I emphasized the concept that we are on our own individual path, and we must each persevere in making it to the Tree where we may reunite with family in worship of the Lord.

After sharing my thoughts, Covey remarked: "With all due respect, Mother, we are not on the path alone. We walk hand in hand with God and with one another along the way. And the path for each individual is not always straight and narrow. Some of us may let go of the rod, or are led off of the path, temporarily, due to temptation or diversion. But as family members, we are there to buoy up, to redirect steps, to help one another stay on the path and hold fast to the rod. The support of the family and of our Heavenly Father is what assists us in making it to the Tree. We are not alone." How true those words have proven to be.

The path of discipleship

To my understanding, discipleship is about coming unto Christ, following His example and teachings, and freely partaking of the fruit of the Tree of Life (see Alma 5:34). I am always on the lookout for applications that connect Lehi's Dream to discipleship, whether implied or overt. Below are two of my favorites:

- "Lehi's dream in the *Book of Mormon* identifies the path we should follow, the challenges we will encounter, and the spiritual resources available to assist us in following and coming unto the Savior. Pressing forward on the strait and narrow path is what He would have us do. Tasting the fruit of the tree and becoming deeply "converted unto the Lord" are the blessings He yearns for us to receive. Hence, He beckons us, 'Come, follow me.'"[5]

- "When you walk the path of discipleship—when you move toward Heavenly Father—there is something within you that will confirm that you have heard the call of the Savior and set your heart toward the light. It will tell you that you are on the right path and that you are returning home.

  "You cannot just float in the waters of life and trust that the current will take you wherever you hope to be one day. Discipleship requires our willingness to swim upstream when needed.

  "No one else is responsible for your personal journey. The Savior [and your fellow Saints] will help you and prepare the way before you, but the commitment to follow Him and keep His commandments must come from you. That is your sole burden, your sole privilege. This is your great adventure."[6]

Through the mists of darkness that seek to derail us along the path of discipleship, the laughing and mocking directed towards those who uphold God's doctrines and standards, and the bare-knuckled effort required in making it to the Tree, we arrive at our intended destination exhausted yet worshipful. "For the Lord God will help me, therefore shall I not be confounded. Therefore, have I set my face like a flint, and I know that I shall not be ashamed" (2 Ne. 7:7).

Spiritual Confidence/Certitude

I have a close friend who is currently serving as the Relief Society president in her ward. Not long ago, she administered a survey to the members of her Relief Society asking them to name their deepest concerns and worries for the future. Her purpose in gathering this information was to help fashion their Sunday curriculum to best meet the needs of the sisters.

Not surprisingly, this leader found that the deepest apprehensions the sisters had was about their families—primarily, the strength of their marriages, the conversion of their children, and the influence of the world upon their family members. What did surprise her, however, was to discover how many sisters expressed a lack of spiritual confidence and anxiety about remaining strong and true to the faith.

To me, a ward Relief Society is a microcosm of the sisters in the worldwide Church, and local concerns are often applicable universally—for that which is most personal is most general.

Contemplating these findings reminded me of the time when I was serving in our stake Young Women's presidency. Prior to general conference, the General Young Women's Presidency invited local ward and stake presidencies to the Tabernacle on Temple Square for some much-needed training.

I distinctly remember Sister Susan Tanner, the Young Women General President at the time, talking about the need to strengthen the spiritual confidence and certitude of the young women of the Church. She mentioned that without spiritual confidence, our young women would not be able to stand against the adversary; but with such certitude, they would have the power to remain strong.

Sister Tanner then proceeded to share three principles that, if understood, would help the young women gain spiritual confidence. They were:

1. Identity
2. Worthiness
3. Support

Just as local needs may be universally applicable, so too may principles taught to the young women be applied to the general membership of the Church. It is vital for each of us to gain an understanding of our true identity, to be worthy of the guidance of the Holy Spirit, and to receive support from fellow members of the Church and from our Heavenly Father. When these conditions are met, they bolster spiritual confidence and inspire certitude.

Identity

In preparation for Mother's Day, my sister-in-law, Jeri, shared an article with our family from a Latter-day Saint blogger named Dustin Phelps. In his article, he clarifies that God holds a grander view of womanhood than any of us could ever imagine. He introduces the Hebrew word, "Eben-Ezer," and explains that it means strength or defender/protector. He says that this word is used two dozen times in the Old Testament, and it almost always describes God in a military context, such as a Divine Helper or Protector—except when referring to Eve.

Concerning Eve, Genesis 2:18 reads: "And the Lord God said, it is not good that the man should be alone; [so] I will make him a *help meet* for him." In studying the etymology of "help meet," Brother Phelps found that the original Hebrew translation interprets the latter half of the term "meet" as "Ezer"— which is a combination of two source words: one which means strength, and another which translates to rescuing, saving, and defending.[7]

On close examination of the scriptural context, Brother Phelps points out that the Lord Himself is referred to as an "Ezer," particularly during times when Israel is too weak to stand against its enemies alone. In a similar manner, he asserts that Eve is considered to be an "Ezer," as God recognizes that Adam cannot live without her. Eve is Adam's first friend, partner, ally, and strength in doing battle with evil and fulfilling God's purposes on the earth.

Brother Phelps concludes his article with the following summation:

"So, the very verse that has been used to marginalize women [as a 'helpmeet'], was really God's own tribute to His daughters. It is high time that we reclaimed and embraced God's vision of women . . .

"So, the next time you read Genesis 2:18 and you are tempted to imagine a submissive housekeeper, instead think of a warrior with a drawn sword. Think of a change maker. Think of a leader. Think of an aunt, a sister, a daughter, a friend, a mother, a wife, a young women's leader, or Sunday school teacher."[8]

There is no one more powerful or influential than a

converted woman who knows who she is, what she stands for, and who is prepared to do battle for the cause of Christ. A woman like that can change the world.

Sister Sheri Dew declared: "The moment we learn to unleash the full influence of converted, covenant-keeping women, the kingdom of God will change overnight."9 How can we come to such a moment?

Worthiness

To obtain spiritual confidence, worthiness is key. When we are worthy of and qualify for the presence of the Holy Ghost, "then shall [our] *confidence* wax strong in the presence of God," and the "Holy Ghost shall be [our] constant companion . . ." (D&C 121:45-46). But without such worthiness, we have no promise.

Not long ago, I had an experience with this principle when my husband, Dave, and I returned to Ireland to visit our mission. We had both served in the Ireland Dublin Mission (at different times), and now we had a daughter and her husband, Hannah and Taylor, who were living and working in Dublin. It provided just the impetus we needed to return to our beloved country.

We purposely arranged our visit to fall over a Sunday because we wished to attend two different wards in Dublin in an attempt to meet as many former friends and ward members as possible. The first ward we attended was the Finglas Ward in north Dublin. As a missionary, Dave had actually lived across the street from the church and had helped build the meetinghouse, so it was a tender mercy for him to see his old flat and to witness how the ward had flourished.

For me, I was hoping to see one of the investigators I had taught many years before. The last time I had been in that building, it pained me to say goodbye to Paschal—a 20-year-old young man I had helped teach over a nine-month period. Paschal had felt of the power of the Holy Ghost, had obtained a testimony of the gospel of Jesus Christ and the *Book of Mormon*, but he did not possess—at the time—the spiritual confidence needed to be baptized.

After I left the mission field and my companion went home the month following, Paschal lost contact with the Church and the missionaries. However, about eight months after returning home, I received a letter from the sister missionaries in the "Raheny House" where I had lived in Dublin, informing me that Paschal was going to be baptized! They explained that he called the house one day, introduced himself, and with resolve declared that he wanted to be baptized.

Paschal went on to explain to the sisters that he had been taught by the missionaries, he knew the Church was true, and he had felt the "power" of the Holy Ghost on an intermittent basis. He realized that he could no longer live without that power in his life. Come what may, he desired to receive the "gift" of the Holy Ghost so that he "may always have his Spirit to be with [him]" (see Moroni 4:3).

Now, these many years later, I was sitting on the front row in the Finglas Ward chapel when the sacrament meeting program was announced. Paschal and his wife were to be the speakers! They stood up, and with conviction, bore powerful testimony of how the Church today is the same church that Christ organized when he was on the earth.

To see Paschal as a faithful member of the Church, sealed in the temple to a spiritually strong and beautiful sister, was an overwhelming blessing. I felt as Alma did, when, after a separation of fourteen years, he was astonished to encounter the sons of Mosiah—and "what added more to his joy, they were still his brethren in the Lord" (Alma 17:2).

The spiritual confidence that Paschal radiated was a result of his worthiness in qualifying for the gift of the Holy Ghost. Just as he had desired, "the Holy Ghost [had become his] constant companion . . ." (see D&C 121:46).

Support

As sisters of the Relief Society, we have been asked to minister to one another—to assess the needs of those around us, and then act upon the promptings of the Spirit. The support we give to our fellow brothers and sisters in the Church is crucial to strengthening their faith and capacity. Just as Alma instructed his people, we are to "watch over [our] people, and . . . nourish them with things pertaining to righteousness" (Mosiah 23:18).

General Relief Society president, Sister Jean Bingham, taught the importance of ministering and lending support: "The Savior is our example in everything—not only in what we should do but *why* we should do it. His life on earth was [an] invitation to us—to raise our sights a little higher, to forget our own problems and [to] reach out to others."[10]

In an interview with the *Deseret News*, Boston Marathon 2nd place finisher, 26-year-old Sarah Sellers, tells how she was able to persist in the 26.2-mile race, and ultimately triumph, due to the gospel perspective revealed to her along the way.

Despite "monsoon-like" weather conditions, Sarah discovered a meaningful parallel for running the race of life. As she ran through a torrent of freezing wind and rain, she discovered that she literally "drew strength" from the positive energy of the spectators who lined the route and cheered her on.

A scripture came to mind about how God promised to send angels to support His children in their trials—and in the midst of her ordeal, she found this to be true:

"And whoso receiveth you, there I will be also, for I will go before your face. I will be on your right hand and on your left, and my Spirit shall be in your hearts, and mine angels round about you, to bear you up (D&C 84:88)."

Sarah insists that her experience running the Boston Marathon is analogous to the human experience. During the second half of the race when she was really struggling and was tempted to slow her pace, she would engage the spectators by throwing a fist pump or a wave into the crowd. They responded with enthusiasm and encouragement, which gave her the courage and strength to keep going. In Sarah's words:

"We're in the elements, we're suffering, and we feel the pain at the moment. But really there are cheerleaders on both sides to buoy us up the entire time. If you are looking at the pavement, focused on the fact that you're getting freezing rain from all angles, it's easy to get down on yourself and feel alone.

"In the spiritual sense, we're never alone, even if it feels like it. It's probably because we're looking down at the pavement. We need to face forward, focus on our goals, think about the reason we are there, and draw upon the support of our faith and our people."[11]

What ultimately gave Sarah hope and spiritual confidence was when she looked around to see that God had sent His angels to support and strengthen her.

The destiny of the Lord's work: Ensign Peak

On July 26, 1847, just two days after the Mormon Pioneers entered the Salt Lake Valley, Brigham Young and seven of his associates climbed a dome-shaped peak, which stood about a mile north of where the Utah State Capitol building now stands. Before leaving Nauvoo, Brigham Young was given a vision of the Prophet Joseph wherein he was shown the peak and the Salt Lake Valley.

Wilford Woodruff was the first to ascend the peak, Brigham Young the last, due to a recent illness. It was suggested that this would be a fitting place to "set up an ensign for the nations" where the Lord "shall assemble the outcasts of Israel, and gather together the dispersed of Judah from the four corners of the earth," as foretold in Isaiah 11:12. It was then named Ensign Peak, and in later years a standard was erected on its summit.[12]

In speaking of this historic occasion, President Gordon B. Hinckley said:

"How foolish, someone might have said, had he heard these men that July morning of 1847. They did not look like statesmen with great dreams. They did not look like rulers poring over maps and planning an empire. They were exiles, driven from their fair city on the Mississippi [River] into this desert region of the West. But they were possessed of a vision drawn from the scriptures and words of revelation.

"I marvel at the foresight of that little group. It was both audacious and bold. It was almost unbelievable. Here they were, almost a thousand miles [1,600 kilometers] from the nearest settlement to the east and almost eight hundred miles [1,300 kilometers] from the Pacific Coast. They were in an untried climate. The soil was different from that of the black loam of Illinois and Iowa, where they had most recently lived. They had never raised a crop here. They had never experienced a winter. They had not built a structure of any kind.

"These prophets, dressed in old, travel-worn clothes, standing in boots they had worn for more than a thousand miles from Nauvoo to this valley, spoke of a millennial vision. They spoke out of a prophetic view of the marvelous destiny of this cause. They came down from the peak that day and went to work to bring reality to their dream."[13]

Missionaries who serve in Scotland experience something similar when they arrive in the mission field. They are taken to "Pratt's Hill," named for Elder Orson Pratt, who climbed a hill above Edinburgh Castle in May of 1840, to dedicate Scotland for the preaching of the gospel. Elder Pratt foresaw a remarkable future for the Church in that beautiful land, and when the missionaries visit this historic site, they are invited to assist in fulfilling this vision.

Missionaries who serve in Taipei experience something comparable upon their arrival in Taiwan. After departing the plane, the first stop made is to the beautiful Grand Hotel, decorated with more than 13,000 dragons, where, on June 1, 1959, Elder Mark E. Petersen offered a prayer of dedication to the Lord. To be part of this special place is to share in its destiny.

Whether it be at Ensign Peak in Salt Lake City, Utah, Pratt's Hill in Edinburgh, Scotland, or the Grand Hotel in Taipei, Taiwan, these hilltop monuments inspire us to remember our roots of faith. They give us a vision of the great and marvelous work of salvation that is unfolding and help us visualize *our role* in its hastening.

The mission of the Church

When Gordon B. Hinckley was the President of the Church (1995-2008), he declared that as members of the Church it was our duty to do our part to help bring the Church of Jesus Christ of Latter-day Saints "out of obscurity" (D&C 1:30). He clearly defined what our purpose as a church should be:

"I believe and testify that it is *the mission of this Church* to stand as an ensign to the nations and a light to the world. We have had placed upon us a great, all-encompassing mandate from which we cannot shrink nor turn aside. We accept that mandate and are determined to fulfill it, and with the help of God we shall do it."[14]

A generous God has poured out a flood of light and truth upon the Latter-day Saints to the extent that we have been blessed with "the Malachi measure: 'There [is] not . . . room enough to receive it.'"[15] In response to these blessings, President Dieter F. Uchtdorf has asked Church members to ponder, and then to act upon, this compelling question: "What shall we give in return for so much?"[16]

"Choose to be one of His true disciples now"

In a Facebook post on July 28, 2017, President Russell M. Nelson, now our beloved prophet, wrote the following expression about discipleship:

"In a coming day, you will present yourself before the Savior. You will be overwhelmed to the point of tears to be in His holy presence. You will struggle to find words to thank Him for paying for your sins, for forgiving you of any unkindness toward others, for healing you from the injuries and injustices of this life.

"You will thank Him for strengthening you to do the impossible, for turning your weaknesses into strengths, and for making it possible for you to live with Him and your family forever. His identity, His Atonement, and His attributes will become personal and real to you.

"But you don't have to wait until then. Choose to be one of His true disciples now. Be one who truly loves Him, who truly wants to serve and lead as He did."

True discipleship requires a fully consecrated heart and mind and our very best efforts—for the Lord Jesus Christ is the One we are seeking to emulate, and it is by *His* grace that we are ultimately saved.

"Come unto the Holy One of Israel, and feast upon that which perisheth not" (see 2 Nephi 9: 51), even the fruit of the Tree of Life, "which is most precious, which is sweet above all that is sweet, and which is white above all that is white, yea, and pure above all that is pure; and ye shall feast upon this fruit even until ye are filled, that ye hunger not, neither shall ye thirst" (see Alma 32:42).

I testify that this is the Lord's Church, restored through the Prophet Joseph Smith—of this I am sure.

Initiatives to consider

1. What does President Packer mean by his statement, "Lehi's dream has in it *everything* a Latterday Saint needs to understand the test of life"? What special meaning does Lehi's Dream have for you?

2. How can you gain greater spiritual confidence and certitude?

3. Think of an "Ensign Peak" experience you have had when you caught a glimpse or a vision of the destiny of the Lord's Church. Ponder on your role in hastening the work of salvation.

---

[1] Boyd K. Packer, "Finding Ourselves in Lehi's Dream," *Ensign*, Aug. 2010.

[2] David A. Bednar, "Lehi's Dream: Holding Fast to the Rod," *Ensign*, Oct. 2011.

[3] Boyd K. Packer, "Finding Ourselves in Lehi's Dream," *Ensign*, Aug. 2010.

[4] David A. Bednar, "Lehi's Dream: Holding Fast to the Rod," *Ensign*, Oct. 2011.

[5] David A. Bednar, "If Ye Had Known Me," *Ensign*, Nov. 2016.

[6] Dieter F. Uchtdorf, "A Yearning for Home," *Ensign*, Nov. 2017.

[7] Dustin Phelps, "God's Hidden Tribute to Mother Eve: This Will Change the Way You See Womanhood," *Happiness-Seekers.com*, 30 Apr. 2018.

[8] *Ibid.*

[9] Sheri Dew, *Women and the Priesthood: What One Mormon Woman Believes* (Deseret Book, 2013), 163.

[10] Jean B. Bingham, "Ministering as the Savior Does," *Ensign*, May 2018.

[11] Trent Toone, "Why Sarah Sellers Says Her 2nd Place Boston Marathon Run Brought to Mind an LDS Scripture," *Deseret News*, 19 Apr. 2018.

[12] Information taken from Ensign Peak marker.

[13] Gordon B. Hinckley, *Teachings of Presidents of the Church: Gordon B. Hinckley* (The Church of Jesus Christ of Latter-day Saints, 2016), 58-60.

[14] *Ibid*, 57.

[15] Neal A. Maxwell, *We Shall Prove Them Herewith* (Deseret Book, 1982), 28-29.

[16] Dieter F. Uchtdorf, "O How Great the Plan of Our God," *Ensign*, Nov. 2016.

Conclusion

. . . be ready always to give an answer to every man that asketh you a reason of the hope that is in you. . .

— 1 Peter 3:15

The more deeply we become converted, the greater our desire to share what we know to be true and to reveal the source of these convictions.

President Gordon B. Hinckley was a model of someone who felt a special reverence for the people and places involved in the restoration of the gospel and who boldly shared its message throughout his life. This willingness grew from a deep gratitude for the Lord and His Prophet into "an ever-growing compulsion to bear testimony of the divinity of the Lord and of the mission of the Prophet Joseph Smith."[1] In other words, he was valiant in the testimony of Jesus and in His restored gospel.

There are countless examples from the *Book of Mormon*, which also illustrate this principle—Lehi's partaking of the fruit of the Tree of Life, Enos's praying through the night for the welfare of his brethren, Alma's response to Abinadi's teachings, Alma the Younger and the four sons of Mosiah preaching the gospel to the Lamanites, the Anti-Nephi-Lehi's love towards those who sought to destroy them, and Moroni and the motivation behind his affirming "promise"—to name a few.

As Elder Ballard taught, "A most significant evidence of our conversion and of how we feel about the gospel in our own lives is our willingness to share it with others."[2]

President Hinckley often pleaded with the members of the Church to "open your mouths," and to "stand for something." He implored:

"I urge you with all the capacity that I have to reach out in a duty that stands beyond the requirements of our everyday lives; that is, to stand strong, even to become a leader in speaking up in behalf of those causes which make our civilization shine and which give comfort and peace to our lives.

"You can be a leader. You must be a leader, as a member of this Church, in those causes for which this Church stands. Do not let fear overcome your efforts. We have nothing to fear. God is at the helm."[3]

Indeed, God *is* at the helm, and sharing our converted voices can and will make a difference. Sisters throughout the ages have demonstrated a faithful pattern of discipleship that we would do well to follow. In *Daughters in My Kingdom: The History of the Relief Society,* it reads:

"The New Testament includes accounts of women, named and unnamed, who exercised faith in Jesus Christ, learned and lived His teachings, and testified of His ministry, miracles, and majesty. These women became exemplary disciples and important witnesses in the work of salvation."[4]

We, too, may become "exemplary disciples and important witnesses in the work of salvation" by being true to what we know to be true and standing for truth and righteousness. Like the early Saints, our mandate as converted Latter-day Saint women, and what we can give in return for so much, is to stand as witnesses for the Lord, His Church, and His prophets—past and present.

When I consider the divinely appointed responsibility with which we have been charged—to shine as a light to the nations of the world—I cannot help but feel compelled to lend my voice, my time, my talents, all that I am, and everything the Lord has blessed me with, to this great and marvelous work of salvation.

---

[1] Gordon B. Hinckley, *Teachings of Presidents of the Church: Gordon B. Hinckley* (The Church of Jesus Christ of Latter-day Saints, 2016), 43.

[2] M. Russell Ballard, "Now Is the Time," *Ensign*, Nov. 2000.

[3] Gordon B. Hinckley, *Teachings of Presidents of the Church: Gordon B. Hinckley* (The Church of Jesus Christ of Latter-day Saints, 2016), 64.

[4] *Daughters in My Kingdom: The History of the Relief Society* (The Church of Jesus Christ of Latter-day Saints, 2011), 3.

Selected Bibliography

Alexander, Eben. *Proof of Heaven: A Neurosurgeon's Journey into the Afterlife.* New York: Simon & Schuster, 2012.

Benson, Ezra Taft. *Teachings of Ezra Taft Benson.* Salt Lake City: Bookcraft, 1988.

Busche, F. Enzio. *Yearning for the Living God.* Salt Lake City: Deseret Book, 2004.

Caldwell, Bo. *City of Tranquil Light.* New York: St. Martin's Griffin, 2010.

Cannon, George Q. *Gospel Truth: Discourses and Writings of President George Q. Cannon, Vol. 1.* Salt Lake City: Deseret Book, 1974.

Covey, Sean. *Fourth Down and Life to Go: How to Turn Life's Setbacks into Triumphs.* Salt Lake City: Bookcraft, 1990.

Covey, Sean. *The 6 Most Important Decisions You'll Ever Make.* New York: Fireside, 2006.

Covey, Stephen R. *Primary Greatness.* New York: Simon & Schuster, 2015.

Covey, Stephen R. *The 7 Habits of Highly Effective People.* New York: Simon & Schuster, 1989.

_____. *Daughters in My Kingdom: The History of the Relief Society*. Salt Lake City: The Church of Jesus Christ of Latter-day Saints, 2011.

de Ruyter-Bons, Kitty. *As I Have Loved You*. Salt Lake City: Covenant, 2003.

Dew, Sheri. *Women and the Priesthood: What One Mormon Woman Believes*. Salt Lake City: Deseret Book, 2013.

Graham, Martha. *This I Believe: The Personal Philosophies of Remarkable Men and Women*. New York: Henry Holt, 2006.

Hinckley, Gordon B. *Discourses, Volume 1: 1995-1999*. Salt Lake City: Deseret Book, 2005.

Hinckley, Gordon B. *Teachings of Presidents of the Church: Gordon B. Hinckley*. Salt Lake City: The Church of Jesus Christ of Latter-day Saints, 2016.

Hunter, Howard W. *Teachings of Presidents of the Church: Howard W. Hunter*. Salt Lake City: The Church of Jesus Christ of Latter-day Saints, 2015.

Kushner, Harold. *When All You've Ever Wanted Isn't Enough: The Search for a Life that Matters*. New York: Fireside, 1986.

Madsen, Barnard N. *The Truman G. Madsen Story: A Life*

of Study and Faith. Salt Lake City: Deseret Book, 2016.

Madsen, Truman. *The Temple: Where Heaven Meets Earth*. Salt Lake City: Deseret Book, 2008.

Maxwell, Neal A. *Deposition of a Disciple*. Salt Lake City: Deseret Book, 1976.

Maxwell, Neal A. *Notwithstanding My Weakness*. Salt Lake City: Deseret Book, 1981.

Maxwell, Neal A. *We Shall Prove Them Herewith*. Salt Lake City: Deseret Book, 1982.

McCullough, David. *The American Spirit*. New York: Simon & Schuster, 2017.

Nelson, Wendy Watson. *What Would a Holy Woman Do?* Salt Lake City: Deseret Book, 2013.

Nouwen, Henri L.M. *The Return of the Prodigal Son: A Story of Homecoming*. New York: Doubleday, 1994.

Packer, Boyd K. *Preparing to Enter the Holy Temple*. Salt Lake City: The Church of Jesus Christ of Latter-day Saints, 2002.

Pratt, Parley P. *Journal History of the Church of Jesus Christ of Latter-day Saints*, Nov. 7, 1853.

Ratey, John J. *Spark: The Revolutionary Science of Exercise and the Brain*. New York: Little, Brown and Company,

2008.

Seligman, Martin. *Flourish: A Visionary New Understanding of Happiness and Well-Being*. New York: Atria, 2011.

Shakespeare, William. *As You Like It*. New York: Dover, 2011.

Smith, Hyrum. *What Matters Most: The Power of Living Your Values*. New York: Fireside, 2000.

Smith, Joseph, Jr. *History of the Church*, 4:535–41. The Wentworth Letter was originally published in Nauvoo in the *Times and Seasons*, 1 Mar. 1842, and it also appears in *A Comprehensive History of the Church*, 1:55.

Smith, Joseph, Jr. *Lectures on Faith*. American Fork, UT: Covenant Communications, 2003. The *Lectures on Faith* were originally published in the forepart of the *Doctrine and Covenants* in all editions from 1835 until 1921.

Smith, Joseph F. *Gospel Doctrine: Selections from the Sermons and Writings of Joseph F. Smith*. Salt Lake City: Deseret News, 1919.

Smith, Joseph F. *Teachings of the Presidents of the Church: Joseph F. Smith*. Salt Lake City: The Church of Jesus Christ of Latter-day Saints, 1998.

_____. *Stewards of the Promise: The Heritage of the Latter-day Saints on the Hawaiian Islands of Maui,*

Molokai, and Lanai. Lahaina: Lahaina Stake Presidency of the Church of Jesus Christ of Latter-day Saints.

Wilcox, Brad. *The Continuous Atonement*. Salt Lake City: Deseret Book, 2009.

Wolpe, David. *Making Loss Matter: Creating Meaning in Difficult Times*. New York: Riverhead Books, 1999.

Wooden, John and Don Yaeger. *A Game Plan for Life*. New York: Bloomsbury, 2009.

Acknowledgements

"When the student is ready, the teacher will appear." I have found this saying, attributed to Buddha, to be true to life. Writing this manuscript has been a testament to me that we find what we seek, and we seek what we find. My mind has been so attuned to looking for insightful content applicable to this project, that I find it everywhere: in regular Sunday meetings, in ward, stake, and general conferences, in printed and online periodicals, in conversations, and in life experiences in general. My task as a writer has been to synthesize these impressions into themes that may be applied to the reader's life.

The source material in this book has been directly influenced by people of strong character: primarily, from the lifetime of gospel teaching and example of my parents, my siblings, my husband, and my children; shared conversations and lessons learned from individuals in my neighborhood, stake, and book group, as well as from life-long friends and family members.

In short, as Joshua Wooden (Coach John Wooden's father) taught his children: "There is nothing you know that you haven't learned from someone else."[1] I fully admit this to be the case, and I have attempted to cite whatever resources I draw from in this manuscript.

More than any other source, however, my Heavenly Father has provided me with constant inspiration and guidance throughout this entire process. Like Nephi, "I

---

[1] Don Yaeger, *A Game Plan for Life: The Power of Mentoring* (Bloomsbury, 2009), 11.

know in whom I have trusted. My God hath been my support" (2 Nephi 4:19-20). With all of my heart, I acknowledge His hand in my life.

About Atmosphere Press

Atmosphere Press is an independent, full-service publisher for excellent books in all genres and for all audiences. Learn more about what we do at atmospherepress.com.

We encourage you to check out some of Atmosphere's latest releases, which are available at Amazon.com and via order from your local bookstore:

Great Spirit of Yosemite: The Story of Chief Tenaya, nonfiction by Paul Edmondson

My Cemetery Friends: A Garden of Encounters at Mount Saint Mary in Queens, New York, nonfiction and poetry by Vincent J. Tomeo

Change in 4D, nonfiction by Wendy Wickham

Disruption Games: How to Thrive on Serial Failure, nonfiction by Trond Undheim

Eyeless Mind, nonfiction by Stephanie Duesing

A Blameless Walk, nonfiction by Charles Hopkins

The Horror of 1888, nonfiction by Betty Plombon

White Snake Diary, nonfiction by Jane P. Perry

From Rags to Rags, essays by Ellie Guzman

Giving Up the Ghost, essays by Tina Cabrera

Family Legends, Family Lies, nonfiction by Wendy Hoke

About the Author

Maria Covey Cole is a frequent speaker and presenter and the author of *Contentment: Inspiring Insights for Latter-day Saint Mothers,* published by Covenant Communications in 2009, and a co-author and/or editor of several other books. She holds a bachelor's degree in English from Brigham Young University, and a master's degree in Educational Studies from the University of Utah.

She has been a copy editor at Bookcraft Publishers, the director of the Sylvan Learning Center in Salt Lake City, and has taught classes at BYU-Provo, BYU-Hawaii, the University of Utah, and most recently, LDS Business College (newly renamed Ensign College).

Maria is the proud co-founder of the *Excellent Women Book Club,* which is still going strong after nearly three decades. She finds contentment in reading, writing, and teaching—and along with her husband Dave—raising their five children and a growing number of grandchildren.